The Third Way

Anthony Giddens

THE THIRD WAY

The Renewal of Social Democracy

Polity

First published in 1998 by Polity Press in association with Blackwell Publishers Ltd.

Reprinted 1998 twice, 1999 three times, 2000 four times, 2001

Editorial office:
Polity Press
65 Bridge Street
Cambridge CB2 1UR, UK

Published in the USA by
Blackwell Publishers Inc.
350 Main Street
Malden, MA 02148, USA

Marketing and production:
Blackwell Publishers Ltd
108 Cowley Road
Oxford OX4 1JF, UK

A CIP catalogue record for this book is available from the British Library.

Library of Congress Cataloging-in-Publication Data

Giddens, Anthony.
   The third way : the renewal of social democracy / Anthony Giddens.
      p.   cm.
   Includes index.
   ISBN 0–7456–2266–6 — ISBN 0–7456–2267–4 (pbk.)
   1. Post-communism.   2. Socialism.   3. Welfare state.   4. Right and left (Political science)   I. Title.
   HX73.G55   1999
   335—dc21   98–40806
                                                                      CIP

Typeset in 11 on 14pt Sabon
By Wearset, Boldon, Tyne and Wear
Printed in Great Britain by TJ International Ltd, Padstow, Cornwall

This book is printed on acid-free paper.

Contents

v

Contents

Preface

I intend this short book as a contribution to the debate now going on in many countries about the future of social democratic politics. The reasons for the debate are obvious enough – the dissolution of the 'welfare consensus' that dominated in the industrial countries up to the late 1970s, the final discrediting of Marxism and the very profound social, economic and technological changes that helped bring these about. What should be done in response, and whether social democracy can survive at all as a distinctive political philosophy, are much less obvious.

I believe social democracy can not only survive, but prosper, on an ideological as well as a practical level. It can only do so, however, if social democrats are prepared to revise their pre-existing views more thoroughly than most have done so far. They·need to find a third way. As I explain in the text, the term 'third way' is of no particular significance in and of itself. It has been used many times before in the past history of social democracy, and also by writers and politicians of quite different political persuasions. I make use of it here to refer to social democratic renewal – the present-day version of the periodic rethinking that social democrats have had to carry out quite often over the past century.

In Britain 'third way' has come to be associated with the politics of Tony Blair and New Labour. Tony Blair's political beliefs have frequently been compared to those of the New Democrats in the US, and indeed there have been close and direct contacts between New Labour and the New Democrats. It has been said that 'like the Thatcher and Major governments, the Blair government looks across the Atlantic for inspiration, not across the channel. Its rhetoric is American, the intellectual influences which have shaped its project are American; its political style is American.'[1]

The statement is not wholly true. Labour's welfare to work programme, for instance, may have an American-style label, but arguably draws its inspiration more from Scandinavian active labour market programmes than from the US. In so far as the observation is valid, however, the emphasis is one that needs correcting. The debate around New Labour, lively and interesting though it is, has been carried on largely in ignorance of comparable discussions that have been going on in Continental social democracy for some while. Tony Blair's break with old Labour was a significant accomplishment, but a similar sort of break has been made by virtually all Continental social democratic parties.

In many respects the debate in the UK needs to catch up with the more advanced sectors of Continental social democracy. Yet the UK is also in a position to contribute actively to the new ideas now emerging. Rather than merely appropriating American trends and notions, Britain could be a sparking point for creative interaction between the US and Continental Europe. Most countries on the Continent have not experienced lengthy periods of neoliberal government as the UK has. Whatever else Thatcherism may or may not have done, it certainly shook up British society. Margaret Thatcher, like most other neoliberals, was no ordinary conservative. Flying the flag of free markets, she attacked established institutions and elites, while her policies lent further force to changes already sweeping through the society at large. The Labour Party and its intellectual sympathizers first of all responded largely by reaffirming old left views. The electoral setbacks the party suffered by so doing, however, necessarily stimulated a new orientation. As a consequence, political discussion in the UK in some ways has been more free thinking than in social democratic circles on the Continent. Ideas developed in Britain could have direct relevance to the Continental debates, as these have mostly unfolded against a different backdrop.

This book grew out of a series of informal evening discussion meetings between myself, Ian Hargreaves and Geoff Mulgan, both of whom I would like to thank. Originally we were going to produce a collective document about the revival of social democracy. For various reasons this didn't materialize, but I have drawn much inspiration from our meetings. I must especially thank David Held, who meticulously read several versions of the manuscript and whose comments were crucial for the restructuring of the text that

I subsequently carried out. Among others who helped me a great deal are Martin Albrow, Ulrich Beck, Alison Cheevers, Miriam Clarke, Amanda Goodall, Fiona Graham, John Gray, Steve Hill, Julian Le Grand, David Miliband, Henrietta Moore and Anne Power. I owe a particular debt to Alena Ledeneva, who not only contributed extensively to the book as a whole but prompted me to continue whenever I became discouraged – which was quite often.

1

Socialism and After

In February 1998, following a policy seminar with the American leadership in Washington, Tony Blair spoke of his ambition to create an international consensus of the centre-left for the twenty-first century. The new approach would develop a policy framework to respond to change in the global order. 'The old left resisted that change. The new right did not want to manage it. We have to manage that change to produce social solidarity and prosperity.'[1] The task is a formidable one because, as these statements indicate, pre-existing political ideologies have lost their resonance.

A hundred and fifty years ago Marx wrote that 'a spectre is haunting Europe' – the spectre of socialism or communism. This remains true, but for different reasons from those Marx had in mind. Socialism and communism have passed away, yet they remain to haunt us. We cannot just put aside the values and ideals that drove them, for some remain intrinsic to the good life that it is the point of social and economic development to create. The challenge is to make these values count where the economic programme of socialism has become discredited.

Political ideas today seem to have lost their capacity to inspire and political leaders their ability to lead. Public debate is dominated by worries about declining moral standards, growing divisions between rich and poor, the stresses of the welfare state. The only groups which appear resolutely optimistic are those that place their faith in technology to resolve our problems. But technological change has mixed consequences, and in any case technology cannot provide a basis for an effective political programme. If political thinking is going to recapture its inspirational qualities, it has to be neither simply reactive nor confined to the everyday and the parochial. Political life is nothing without ideals, but ideals are empty if they don't relate to real possibilities. We need to know both what sort of society we would like to create and the concrete means of moving towards it. This book seeks to show how these aims can be achieved and political idealism revived.

My main point of reference is Britain, although many of my arguments range more widely. In the UK, as in many other countries at the moment, theory lags behind practice. Bereft of the old certainties, governments claiming to represent the left are creating policy on the hoof. Theoretical flesh needs to be put on the skeleton of their policy-making – not just to endorse what they are doing, but to provide politics with a greater sense of direction and purpose. For the left, of course, has always been linked to socialism and, at least as a system of economic management, socialism is no more.

The death of socialism

The origins of socialism were tied up with the early development of industrial society, somewhere in the mid to late eighteenth century. The same is true of its principal opponent, conservatism, which was shaped in reaction to the French Revolution. Socialism began as a body of thought opposing individualism; its concern to develop a critique of capitalism only came later. Before it took on a very specific meaning with the rise of the Soviet Union, communism overlapped heavily with socialism, each seeking to defend the primacy of the social or the communal.

Socialism was first of all a philosophical and ethical impulse, but well before Marx it began to take on the clothing of an economic doctrine. Marx it was, however, who provided socialism with an elaborated economic theory. He also placed socialism in the context of an encompassing account of history. Marx's basic position came to be shared by all socialists, no matter how sharp their other differences. Socialism seeks to confront the limitations of capitalism in order to humanize it or to overthrow it altogether. The economic theory of socialism depends upon the idea that, left to its own devices, capitalism is economically inefficient, socially divisive and unable to reproduce itself in the long term.

The notion that capitalism can be humanized

3

through socialist economic management gives socialism whatever hard edge it possesses, even if there have been many different accounts of how such a goal might be achieved. For Marx, socialism stood or fell by its capacity to deliver a society that would generate greater wealth than capitalism and spread that wealth in more equitable fashion. If socialism is now dead, it is precisely because these claims have collapsed. They have done so in singular fashion. For some quarter of a century following World War II, socialist planning seemed here to stay in both West and East. A prominent economic observer, E.F.M. Durbin, wrote in 1949, 'we are all Planners now ... The collapse of the popular faith in laisser faire has proceeded with spectacular rapidity ... all over the world since the War.'[2]

Socialism in the West became dominated by social democracy – moderate, parliamentary socialism – built upon consolidating the welfare state. In most countries, including Britain, the welfare state was a creation as much of the right as of the left, but in the post-war period socialists came to claim it as their own. For at least some while, even the much more comprehensive planning adopted in the Soviet-style societies appeared economically effective, if always politically despotic. Successive American governments in the 1960s took seriously the claim that the Soviet Union might overtake the US economically within a further thirty years.

In hindsight, we can be fairly clear why the Soviet Union, far from surpassing the US, fell dramatically behind it, and why social democracy encountered its own crises. The economic theory of socialism was always inadequate, underestimating the capacity of

4

capitalism to innovate, adapt and generate increasing productivity. Socialism also failed to grasp the significance of markets as informational devices, providing essential data for buyers and sellers. These inadequacies only became fully revealed with intensifying processes of globalization and technological change from the early 1970s onwards.

Over the period since the mid-1970s, well before the fall of the Soviet Union, social democracy was increasingly challenged by free market philosophies, in particular by the rise of Thatcherism or Reaganism – more generically described as neoliberalism. During the previous period, the idea of liberalizing markets seemed to belong to the past, to an era that had been superseded. From being widely seen as eccentric, the ideas of Friedrich von Hayek, the leading advocate of free markets, and other free market critics of socialism suddenly became a force to be reckoned with. Neoliberalism made less of an impact upon most countries in Continental Europe than upon the UK, the US, Australia and Latin America. Yet on the Continent as elsewhere, free market philosophies became influential.

The categories of 'social democracy' and 'neoliberalism' are wide, and have encompassed groups, movements and parties of various policies and persuasions. Even though each influenced the other, for example, the governments of Ronald Reagan and Margaret Thatcher followed different policies in some contexts. When Thatcher first came to power, she did not have a fully fledged ideology, which was developed as she went along. Thatcherite policies followed by 'left' parties, as in New Zealand, have put a different cast again upon key policy beliefs. Moreover, neoliberalism has two strands. The main one is conservative – the origin of the term 'the new right'. Neoliberalism became the outlook of many conservative parties the world over. However, there is an important type of thinking associated with free market philosophies that, in contrast to the conservative one, is libertarian on moral as well as economic issues. Unlike the Thatcherite conservatives, for example, libertarians favour sexual freedom or the decriminalizing of drugs.

Social democracy is an even broader and more ambiguous term. I mean by it parties and other groups of the reformist left, including the British Labour Party. In the early post-war period, social democrats from many different countries shared a broadly similar per-spective. This is what I shall refer to as old-style or classical social democracy. Since the 1980s, in response to the rise of neoliberalism and the problems of social-ism, social democrats everywhere have started to break away from this prior standpoint.

Social democratic regimes in practice have varied substantially, as have the welfare systems they have nourished. European welfare states can be divided into four institutional groups, all of which share common historical origins, aims and structures:

- the UK system, which emphasizes social services and health, but tends also to have income-dependent benefits;
- Scandinavian or Nordic welfare states, having a very high tax base, universalist in orientation, providing generous benefits and well-funded state services,

including health care;

- Middle European systems, having a relatively low commitment to social services, but well-resourced benefits in other respects, financed mainly from employment and based upon social insurance contributions;
- Southern systems, similar in form to the Middle European ones, but less comprehensive and paying lower levels of support.[3]

Allowing for these variations, classical social democracy and neoliberalism represent two quite distinct

Classical social democracy (the old left)

Pervasive state involvement in social and economic life
State dominates over civil society
Collectivism
Keynesian demand management, plus corporatism
Confined role for markets: the mixed or social economy
Full employment
Strong egalitarianism
Comprehensive welfare state, protecting citizens 'from cradle to grave'
Linear modernization
Low ecological consciousness
Internationalism
Belongs to bipolar world

Thatcherism, or neoliberalism (the new right)

Minimal government
Autonomous civil society
Market fundamentalism
Moral authoritarianism, plus strong economic
  individualism
Labour market clears like any other
Acceptance of inequality
Traditional nationalism
Welfare state as safety net
Linear modernization
Low ecological consciousness
Realist theory of international order
Belongs to bipolar world

---

political philosophies. I summarize the differences in the two boxes above. Broad-brush comparisons of this sort carry an obvious danger of caricature. Yet the contrasts signalled here are real and important, and the residues of classical social democracy are everywhere still strong.

Old-style social democracy

Old-style social democracy saw free market capitalism as producing many of the problematic effects Marx diagnosed, but believed these can be muted or overcome by state intervention in the marketplace. The state has the obligation to provide public goods that markets cannot deliver, or can do so only in a fractured way. A strong government presence in the economy, and other sectors of society too, is normal and desirable, since public power, in a democratic society, represents the collective will. Collective decision-making, involving government, business and unions, partly replaces market mechanisms.

For classical social democracy, government involvement in family life is necessary and to be applauded. State benefits are vital for rescuing families in need, and the state should step in wherever individuals, for one reason or another, are unable to fend for themselves. With some conspicuous exceptions, old-style social democrats were inclined to be suspicious of voluntary associations. Such groups often do more bad than good because, as compared with state-provided social services, they tend to be unprofessional, erratic and patronizing to those with whom they deal.

John Maynard Keynes, the economic inspiration of the post-war welfare consensus, was not a socialist, yet he shared some of the emphases of Marx and socialism. Like Marx, Keynes regarded capitalism as having irrational qualities, but he believed these could be controlled to save capitalism from itself. Marx and Keynes both tended to take the productivity of capitalism for granted. The fact that Keynesian theory paid relatively little attention to the supply side of the economy fitted well with social democratic preoccupations. Keynes showed how market capitalism could be stabilized through demand management and the creation of a mixed economy. Although he did not favour it, one feature of the mixed economy in Britain was nationalization. Some economic sectors should be taken out of the market, not only because of the deficiencies of markets, but because industries central to the national interest shouldn't be in private hands.

The pursuit of equality has been a major concern of all social democrats, including the British Labour Party. Greater equality is to be achieved by various strategies of levelling. Progressive taxation, for example, via the welfare state, takes from the rich to give to the poor. The welfare state has two objectives: to create a more equal society, but also to protect individuals across the life cycle. The earliest welfare measures, dating from the nineteenth century, were introduced by liberals or conservatives, and were often opposed by organized labour. The post-war welfare state, however, has generally had a strong base among the manual working class, which until twenty years ago was the prime source of electoral support for social democratic parties.

Until the setbacks of the late 1970s, social democracy everywhere followed a linear model of modernization – the 'path of socialism'. Perhaps the most prominent interpreter of the rise of the welfare state in the UK, the sociologist T.H. Marshall, provided a compelling exposition of such a model. The welfare state is the high point of a lengthy process of the evolution of citizenship rights. Like most others in the early post-war period, Marshall expected that welfare systems would progressively expand, matching economic development with the ever-fuller implementation of social rights.

By and large, old-style social democracy did not have

a hostile attitude towards ecological concerns, but found it difficult to accommodate to them. Its corporatist emphasis, its orientation to full employment and its overwhelming stress upon the welfare state made it ill-adapted to confronting ecological issues in a systematic way. Nor in practice did it have a strong global outlook. Social democracy was internationalist in its orientation, looking to create solidarity between like-minded political parties rather than confronting global problems as such. Yet it was strongly bound up with the bipolar world – situated between the welfare minimalism of the US and the command economies of communism.

The neoliberal outlook

Hostility to 'big government', a first and prime characteristic of neoliberal views, comes from several sources. The founding father of conservatism in Britain, Edmund Burke, expressed his distaste for the state, which if expanded too far becomes the enemy of freedom and self-reliance. American conservatism has long been hostile to centralized government. Thatcherism drew upon these ideas, but also upon classical liberal scepticism about the role of the state, based on economic arguments about the superior nature of markets. The thesis of the minimal state is closely bound up with a distinctive view of civil society as a self-generating mechanism of social solidarity. The little platoons of civil society must be allowed to

11

flourish, and will do so if unhampered by state intervention. The virtues of civil society, if left to its own
devices, are said to include 'Good character, honesty,
duty, self-sacrifice, honour, service, self-discipline, tol-
eration, respect, justice, self-improvement, trust, civility, fortitude, courage, integrity, diligence, patriotism,
consideration for others, thrift and reverence'.[4] To the
modern ear, the writer says, these 'have a ring of
antique charm' – but this is because state power has
suppressed them, through sabotaging civil society.

The state, particularly the welfare state, is said to be
destructive of the civil order, but markets are not,
because they thrive on individual initiative. Like the
civil order, if left to themselves markets will deliver the
greatest good to society. Markets 'are perpetual motion
machines, requiring only a legal framework and
government non-interference to deliver uninterrupted
growth'.[5]

Neoliberals link unfettered market forces to a
defence of traditional institutions, particularly the
family and the nation. Individual initiative is to develop
in the economy, but obligations and duties should be
promoted in these other spheres. The traditional family
is a functional necessity for social order, as is the traditional nation. Other family types, such as single-parent
households, or homosexual relationships, only contribute to social decay. Much the same goes for anything that weakens national integrity. Xenophobic
overtones are normally clear in the pronouncements of
neoliberal authors and politicians – they reserve some
of their severest strictures for multiculturalism.

Thatcherism characteristically is indifferent to

inequalities, or actively endorses them. The idea that 'social inequality is inherently wrong or harmful' is 'naive and implausible'.[6] Above all, it is against egalitarianism. Egalitarian policies, most obviously those followed in Soviet Russia, create a society of drab uniformity, and can only be implemented by the use of despotic power. Those closer to liberalism, however, see equality of opportunity as desirable and necessary. This was the sense in which John Major, improbably echoing Marx, spoke of his intention to create a classless society. A society where the market has free play may create large economic inequalities, but these don't matter as long as people with determination and ability can rise to positions that fit their capacities.

Antagonism to the welfare state is one of the most distinctive neoliberal traits. The welfare state is seen as the source of all evils in much the way capitalism once was by the revolutionary left. 'We shall look back on the welfare state with the same contemptuous amusement as that with which we now view slavery as a means of organising effective, motivated work', one writer says. The welfare state 'wreaks enormously destructive harm on its supposed beneficiaries: the vulnerable, the disadvantaged and the unfortunate . . . cripples the enterprising, self-reliant spirit of individual men and women, and lays a depth charge of explosive resentment under the foundations of our free society'.[7]

What provides welfare if the welfare state is to be dismantled? The answer is market-led economic growth. Welfare should be understood not as state benefits, but as maximizing economic progress, and therefore overall wealth, by allowing markets to work their miracles. This orientation normally goes along with a dismissal of ecological problems as scare-stories. Thatcher made a nod in the direction of 'green capitalism', but the usual attitude has been one of hostility. Ecological risks, it has been said, are exaggerated or non-existent – the invention of doom-mongers. The evidence points instead towards an era of greater and more universal prosperity than has ever been known before. This is a linear view of modernization, which almost writes out of court any limits to economic development.

Unlike classical social democracy, neoliberalism is a globalizing theory, and has contributed very directly to globalizing forces. The neoliberals apply at world level the philosophy that guides them in their more local involvements. The world will get along best if markets are allowed to function with little or no interference. As defenders of the traditional nation, however, neoliberals adopt a realist theory of international relations – global society is still a society of nation-states, and in a world of nation-states it is power that counts. Preparedness for war, and the sustaining of military strength, are necessary elements of the role of states in the international system. Like old-style social democracy, neoliberalism developed in the bipolar order and is stamped by the conditions of its origin.

The doctrines compared

Neoliberalism might seem to have triumphed across the world. After all, social democracy is in ideological turmoil, and if fifty years ago everyone was a planner, now no one seems to be. It is a considerable reversal, since for at least a century socialists supposed themselves in the vanguard of history.

Yet rather than standing unchallenged, neoliberalism is in trouble, and it is important to see why. The chief reason is that its two halves – market fundamentalism and conservatism – are in tension. Conservatism always meant a cautious, pragmatic approach to social and economic change – an attitude adopted by Burke in the face of the messianic claims of the French Revolution. The continuity of tradition is central to the idea of conservatism. Tradition contains the accumulated wisdom of the past and therefore supplies a guide to the future. Free market philosophy takes quite a different attitude, pinning its hopes for the future on unending economic growth produced by the liberation of market forces.

Devotion to the free market on the one hand, and to the traditional family and nation on the other, is self-contradictory. Individualism and choice are supposed to stop abruptly at the boundaries of the family and national identity, where tradition must stand intact. But nothing is more dissolving of tradition than the 'permanent revolution' of market forces. The dynamism of market societies undermines traditional structures of authority and fractures local communities; neoliberalism creates new risks and uncertainties which it asks citizens simply to ignore. Moreover, it neglects the social basis of markets themselves, which depend upon the very communal forms that market fundamentalism indifferently casts to the winds.

What of old-style social democracy? We can distinguish a cluster of social traits that the Keynesian welfare consensus took for granted – all of which have subsequently disintegrated:

- a social system, and especially a family form – where the husband was the breadwinner and the wife the housewife and mother – which allowed for an unambiguous definition of full employment;
- a homogeneous labour market where men threatened with unemployment were mostly manual workers willing to do any job at a wage that ensured their survival and that of their families;
- the dominance of mass production in basic sectors of the economy, which tended to create stable, if unrewarding, conditions of work for many in the labour force;
- an elitist state, with small groups of public-spirited experts in the state bureaucracy monitoring the fiscal and monetary policies to be followed;
- national economies that were substantially contained within sovereign boundaries, since Keynesianism presumed the predominance of the domestic economy over external trade in goods and services.[8]

The egalitarianism of the old left was noble in intent, but as its rightist critics say has sometimes led to perverse consequences – visible, for example, in the social engineering which has left a legacy of decaying, crime-ridden housing estates. The welfare state, seen by most as the core of social democratic politics, today creates almost as many problems as it resolves.

The recent debates

Social democratic parties in Europe and elsewhere have been very conscious of these issues, and since at least the early 1980s have been actively responding to them. The need to cut loose from the past received a further dynamic charge from the collapse of East European communism in 1989. Most Western communist parties changed their names and moved closer to social democracy, while in the East European countries new social democratic parties were formed.

In the UK, the first systematic attempt to move away from classical social democratic principles was contained in the Labour Party's Policy Review, established by the Annual Conference in October 1987. Seven review groups were set up, each covering a different area of policy. The review was supposed also to involve the public, but the public meetings were only sparsely attended and in the end played no great role. Confronted by the popular appeal of Thatcherism, there was general agreement among the policy groups that Labour must place greater emphasis on individual freedom and personal choice. Earlier pledges to extend public ownership of industry were discarded, Keynesian demand management was explicitly abandoned, and dependence upon the unions was reduced. Ecological themes were introduced, but these were low-key and were not effectively integrated with the rest of the policy framework.

Similar processes of reform happened in most Continental parties, mainly starting somewhat earlier and sometimes producing more thoroughgoing changes in ideology. Social democratic parties began to concern

17

themselves with issues such as economic productivity, participatory policies, community development and, particularly, ecology. Social democracy 'moved beyond the arena of resource distribution to address the physical and social organisation of production and the cultural conditions of consumption in advanced capitalist societies'.[9]

In Norway, for example, the Labour Party held a 'Freedom Debate' in 1986–8, following a period of Thatcherite government. Six themes were debated in local study groups across the country: the balance between the private and public, flexibility in the working day, educational opportunity, the environment, housing and economic democracy. Arguing for individual interests was no longer considered bad language, and the party was to be 'an open party', through which a diversity of groups could press their demands. A Colombian delegate to a meeting of the Socialist International in 1989 remarked of such a policy shift: 'My party is called liberal, but it's basically quite socialist. With these Europeans it's the other way around.'[10]

Some of the leading Western communist parties made similar changes in the 1980s. The Italian Communist Party was reborn as the Democratic Party of the Left in 1991. Well before that time, however, the party had begun to emphasize themes like those being discussed by the social democratic parties. A major debate began in Italy in the mid-1980s about how far the categories of left and right remain meaningful. Ecological concerns, community participation and constitutional reform came to the fore.

Probably the most significant debates took place in Germany. As elsewhere, the aim was to respond to the rise of free market philosophies, but demand for policy change was also strongly influenced by the presence of a strong green movement. Five years of intense discussion led to a new Basic Programme for the SPD, instituted in the symbolic year of 1989. The programme placed a heavy emphasis on ecological concerns. The German social democrats were the first major social democratic party to seize upon the breakthrough in ecological thinking that happened in the late 1970s. In classical social democratic thinking, it had been assumed that there was a trade-off between economic development and protection of the environment. According to the new theme of ecological modernization, environmental protection is seen as a source of economic growth rather than its opposite.

The Basic Programme also recognized the impact of 'post-materialism' in the developed countries. This is an idea pursued most extensively by the political scientist Ronald Inglehart. After a certain level of prosperity has been reached, it is argued, voters become concerned less with economic issues than with the quality of their lives. The Basic Programme concluded that the outlook of the 'affluent majority' had moved away from the social democratic ethos of collectivism and solidarity. Individual achievement and economic competitiveness had to be brought more to the fore.

Since its landmark Bad Godesberg statement in 1959 the SPD had been committed to the 'discipline of the market'. This was now to be combined with a further retreat from state interventionism. 'For us the state's share is not a dogma . . . the touchstone is whether quality of life is best served by an increase in private consumption or by an improvement in the performance of the state.' The Basic Programme spoke of the need 'to reconcile economic performance with social security' and stressed that 'individuality and solidarity should not be counterposed as opposites'. It concluded that 'So long as important sections of the electorate do not trust the SPD for the tasks of economic modernization, but only for ensuring that social safeguards are maintained, it will be very difficult to build a majority.'[11]

Structures of political support

That these policy shifts were necessary is indicated by changes in patterns of political support, to which all social democratic parties have had to react. The class relations that used to underlie voting and political affiliation have shifted dramatically, owing to the steep decline in the blue-collar working class. The large-scale entry of women into the workforce has further destabilized patterns of class-based support. A sizeable minority no longer votes, and is essentially outside the political process. The party which has grown most over the past few years is one that isn't part of politics at all: the 'non-party of non-voters.'[12] Finally, there is substantial evidence that value changes have occurred, partly as a matter of generational change, and partly in response to other influences.

On this last point, the evidence points to two trends:

a shift, as just suggested, from 'scarcity values' to 'post-materialist values', and a changing distribution of values, which fits neither class lines nor the right/left dichotomy. Although subjected to criticism from many quarters, Inglehart's thesis of value change has received considerable empirical backing.[13] Bringing together survey material from a range of industrial countries, Inglehart shows values of economic achievement and economic growth do fade with increasing prosperity. Self-expression and the desire for meaningful work are replacing the maximizing of economic rewards. These concerns are related to a sceptical attitude towards authority – which can be depoliticizing, but on the whole pushes towards greater democracy and involvement than is currently available in conventional politics.

Social surveys carried out in particular countries confirm the reality of attitude change and the inadequacy of the left/right division as a means of capturing it. John Blundell and Brian Gosschalk, for example, find social and political attitudes in the UK divide into four clusters, which they call conservative, libertarian, socialist and authoritarian. Belief in economic freedom – the free market – is measured on one axis and personal freedom on a second.

The 'conservative' position is the neoliberal one: a conservative favours market freedom, but wants strong state control over issues such as the family, drugs and abortion. 'Libertarians' favour individualism, and low state involvement on all fronts. 'Socialists' are the opposite of conservatives: they want more state intervention in economic life, but are distrustful of markets and are wary of government as far as moral issues are concerned. An 'authoritarian' is someone who wishes the government to have a firm hand in all areas, including both the economic and the moral. The remainder hold a more ambiguous political outlook.

According to the survey data, in the UK about one-third of the population are conservative by these definitions, just under 20 per cent libertarian, 18 per cent socialist, 13 per cent authoritarian and 15 per cent residual. The Labour Party, as reconstructed by Tony Blair, just prior to the 1997 election was in first place for all these groups save the conservatives. Of those intending to vote Conservative, 84 per cent came from two groups, conservatives and libertarians. The results showed very clear differences by age, conforming to the Inglehart thesis: only 18 per cent of the 15–24 age group were conservatives, compared with 54 per cent of the over 55s. Of 15–24-year-olds, 72 per cent agreed with the statement, 'the state has no right to ban any sort of sexual act if it is carried out between consenting adults', while only 36 per cent of those in the over-55 age group did so.[14]

Comparing these findings with research from the US, the polling expert Robert Worcester concludes that:

> characterizations of today's labour and conservative parties . . . as 'left' and 'right' disguise how events affecting both parties over the past two decades have blurred the semantics of yesterday in describing their roles of today . . . the comparison figures between those found in America and New Labour's Britain are remarkable in their consistency, somewhat surprisingly as the ideologies of the two countries have been for the most part very different over the past fifty years.[15]

Comparison of a wider variety of societies shows that patterns of political appeal and support have altered on a very general basis. In virtually all Western countries voting no longer fits class lines, and has ·shifted from a left/right polarization to a more complex picture. The economic axis that used to separate voters into 'socialist' and 'capitalist' positions has much lower salience, while the contrasts of libertarian versus authoritarian, and 'modern' versus 'traditionalist', have grown. Other, more contingent influences – such as leadership style – have become more important than they used to be.

Various dilemmas of political support, but also new possibilities of consensus-building, exist here. Social democratic parties no longer have a consistent 'class bloc' on which to rely. Since they can't depend upon their previous identities, they have to create new ones in a socially and culturally more diverse environment.[16] Even in Sweden, one of the countries where class voting used to be most pronounced, the predictive value of class fell from 53 per cent in 1967 to 34 per cent in 1985. The predictive power of opinions on issues rose steadily over this period; younger and female voters in Sweden are least likely to be influenced by class position.

The fate of social democracy

These changes have not condemned social democrats to a marginal political position. As of mid-1998 social democratic parties or centre-left coalitions are in power in the UK, France, Italy, Austria, Greece and several of the Scandinavian countries among others in Western Europe, while in Eastern Europe they are increasingly prominent.

In spite of their electoral successes social democrats have not yet created a new and integrated political outlook. Social democracy was always linked to socialism. What should its orientation be in a world where there are no alternatives to capitalism? The bipolar world was the context in which post-war social democracy was shaped. Social democrats shared at least some of the perspectives of communism, although they also defined themselves in opposition to it. Does being on the left retain any meaning now that communism has foundered completely in the West and socialism more generally has been dissolved?

The policy debates that took place across Europe in the late 1980s and early 1990s certainly recast social democracy very substantially, but also produced much ideological confusion. A German participant in the SPD's Basic Programme initiative summed up things in an illuminating way:

> The decision to embark on the programme review was taken in a situation in which it is extraordinarily difficult to arrive at a clear picture of developments in the world and in society. That is the dilemma in which the party finds itself. It knows that in these changing times, a reorientation appears necessary but change itself makes reorientation hard to accomplish. Science offers no diagnosis of the age, no common understanding of what is happening and what future developments will be.[17]

In terms of this scenario, what are we to make of talk of a third way? The phrase seems to have originated as early as the turn of the century, and was popular among right-wing groups in the 1920s. Mostly, however, it has been used by social democrats and socialists. In the early post-war period, social democrats quite explicitly thought of themselves as finding a way distinct from American market capitalism and Soviet communism. At the time of its refounding in 1951 the Socialist International explicitly spoke of the third way in this fashion. About twenty years later, as employed by the Czech economist Ota Šik and others, it was used to refer to market socialism. Swedish social democrats seem most often to have spoken of the third way, the last version, in the late 1980s, referring to an important programmatic renewal.

The more recent appropriation of 'third way' by Bill Clinton and Tony Blair has met with a lukewarm reception from most Continental social democrats, as well as from old left critics in their respective countries. The critics see the third way in this guise as warmed-over neoliberalism. They look at the US and see a highly dynamic economy, but also a society with the most extreme levels of inequality in the developed world. Clinton promised to 'end welfare as we know it', seeming to echo some of the attitudes of the neoliberal conservatives. On coming to power, his critics say, Blair and New Labour have persisted with the economic policies of Margaret Thatcher.

My aim in what follows is not to assess whether or not such observations are valid, but to consider where the debate about the future of social democracy stands. I shall take it 'third way' refers to a framework of thinking and policy-making that seeks to adapt social democracy to a world which has changed fundamentally over the past two or three decades. It is a third way in the sense that it is an attempt to transcend both old-style social democracy and neoliberalism.

2

Five Dilemmas

The debates about the future of social democracy over the past ten to fifteen years have raised a diversity of general questions and difficulties – a measure of how problematic the terrain of policies has become. No integrated agenda for social democratic policies can be developed, however, unless at least provisional answers are given to these questions. Here I shall concentrate on five basic dilemmas that have rightly bulked large in the controversies. I shall suggest a view about each, but I have to ask the reader's indulgence. They are all big questions. There is space here only to provide summary answers, and I won't be able to offer enough backing to convince a sceptic in any particular case.

The five dilemmas concern:

- Globalization – what exactly is it and what implications does it have?
- Individualism – in what sense, if any, are modern societies becoming more individualistic?

- Left and right – what are we to make of the claim that they have no meaning any more?
- Political agency – is politics migrating away from orthodox mechanisms of democracy?
- Ecological problems – how should they be integrated into social democratic politics?

Globalization

The history of the unlovely term 'globalization' is an interesting one. Only about ten years ago the word was hardly used in either academic works or the popular press. From being nowhere, the word is everywhere – no political speech is complete, or business manual acceptable, without reference to it. Its new familiarity has prompted intense debate, in academic circles and in the literature of social democracy. It has quite rightly been remarked that in recent years globalization has been at the centre of most political discussions and economic debates.[1]

Most aspects of globalization are disputed: how the term should be understood, whether or not it is new, and what its consequences are likely to be. Two quite contrary views have emerged, to some extent linked to divergent political positions. Some argue that globalization is largely a myth, or is at most a continuation of long-established trends. Unsurprisingly, this stance is attractive to those who wish to defend aspects of old-style social democracy. For them, globalization is an invention of neoliberals. Once we see through the sham, we can carry on much as before. At the other pole are authors and policy-makers who say that globalization is not only real, but already far advanced. As the business guru Keniche Ohmae puts it, we live now in a borderless world, in which the nation-state has become a 'fiction' and where politicians have lost all effective power.[2]

Globalization is ordinarily understood as economic and, as its root suggests, involving connections that span the world. In their book on the subject, Paul Hirst and Graham Thompson put it this way: 'A truly global economy is claimed to have emerged, or to be in the process of emerging, in which distinct national economies and therefore domestic strategies of national economic management are increasingly irrelevant.'[3] They mount an attack on this point of view. Most trade remains regional. For example, the European Union countries trade primarily among themselves. The level of exports from the EU to the rest of the world has only increased marginally over the past three decades. While the US has become more open, to the tune of doubling its exports during the same period, such developments fall well short of creating a 'fully globalized economy'. The advance of trade within and across different economic blocs has simply taken us back to the late nineteenth century. At that time, Hirst and Thompson say, just like today, there was a liberalized trading economy.

This latter point is in fact fairly easily challenged. Even if the current period were only a replay of a century ago, it would still be quite different from the post-war era of the Keynesian welfare state. National economies were more closed then than they are now. In

1950 the export of tradable goods made up only 7 per cent of the GDP of the OECD countries, as compared to 12 per cent in 1911. The 12 per cent level was reached again by 1970, and by 1997 it rose to 17 per cent. Moreover, a much greater range of goods, including many forms of services, is tradable now than was so a century ago. Far more countries are involved in mutual trading arrangements.

The most important change is the expanded role of world financial markets, increasingly operating on a real-time basis. Over a trillion dollars a day is turned over in currency exchange transactions. The proportion of financial exchanges in relation to trade has grown by a factor of five over the past fifteen years.[4] 'Disconnected capital' – institutionally managed money – has increased by 1,100 per cent on a world scale since 1970 in proportion to other forms of capital. Institutional investors based in the US alone held $11.1 trillion in assets in July 1996. Privatized pension funds, or bonds floated to fund pension schemes, are a basic part of this huge sum. In 1995 US pension funds, mutual funds and endowments held $331 billion in institutional equities.[5]

Economic globalization therefore is a reality, and is not just a continuation of, or a reversion to, the trends of previous years. While much trade remains regionalized, there is a 'fully global economy' on the level of financial markets. However, the idea of globalization is misunderstood if it is only applied to connections that are literally world-wide and if it is treated as only, or even primarily, economic. Globalization, as I shall conceive of it in what follows, at any rate, is not only, or even primarily, about economic interdependence, but about the transformation of time and space in our lives. Distant events, whether economic or not, affect us more directly and immediately than ever before. Conversely, decisions we take as individuals are often global in their implications. The dietary habits individuals have, for example, are consequential for food producers, who might live on the other side of the world.

The communications revolution and the spread of information technology are deeply bound up with globalizing processes. This is so even within the economic arena. Twenty-four-hour money markets depend upon a fusion of satellite and computer technologies, affecting many other aspects of society too. A world of instantaneous electronic communication, in which even those in the poorest regions are involved, shakes up local institutions and everyday patterns of life. The influence of television alone is considerable. Most commentators agree, for instance, that the 1989 events in Eastern Europe would not have unfolded in the way in which they did were it not for television.

Is the nation-state becoming a 'fiction', as Ohmae suggests, and government obsolete? They are not, but their shape is being altered. Globalization 'pulls away' from the nation-state in the sense that some powers nations used to possess, including those that underlay Keynesian economic management, have been weakened. However, globalization also 'pushes down' – it creates new demands and also new possibilities for regenerating local identities. The recent upsurge of Scottish nationalism in the UK shouldn't be seen as an isolated example. It is a response to the same structural processes at work elsewhere, such as those in Quebec or Catalonia. Local nationalisms aren't inevitably fragmenting. Quebec may opt out of Canada, as Scotland may out of the UK. Alternatively, each may follow the Catalan route, remaining quasi-autonomous parts of a wider national entity.

Globalization also squeezes sideways, creating new economic and cultural regions that sometimes cross-cut the boundaries of nation-states. Part of Catalonia, and also Spain, Barcelona is involved as well in an economic area that spills over into southern France. The three-way movement of globalization is affecting the position and power of states all over the world. Sovereignty is no longer an all-or-nothing matter, if it ever was: boundaries are becoming fuzzier than they used to be, especially in the context of the European Union. Yet the nation-state is not disappearing, and the scope of government, taken overall, expands rather than diminishes as globalization proceeds. Some nations, in some situations, have more power than they used to have, rather than less – such as the East European countries following the fall of communism.

Nations retain, and will do for the foreseeable future, considerable governmental, economic and cultural power, over their citizens and in the external arena. They will often be able to wield such powers, however, only in active collaboration with one another, with their own localities and regions, and with transnational groups and associations. 'Government' hence becomes less identified with 'the' government – national government – and more wide-ranging.

'Governance' becomes a more relevant concept to refer to some forms of administrative or regulatory capacities. Agencies which either are not part of any government – non-governmental organizations – or are transnational in character contribute to governance.

Globalization is quite often spoken of as if it were a force of nature, but it is not. States, business corporations and other groups have actively promoted its advance. Much of the research that helped create satellite communications was funded by governments, as more recently were the early phases of what has become the internet. Governments have contributed to the expansion of world financial markets through the bonds they have issued to raise money for their domestic commitments. Liberalization and privatization policies have contributed to the intensifying of world trade and economic exchange. Companies have increasingly engaged in direct foreign investment. The sales of the subsidiaries of transnational corporations in 1997 were 20 per cent higher than total world exports of goods and services.

Globalization, in sum, is a complex range of processes, driven by a mixture of political and economic influences. It is changing everyday life, particularly in the developed countries, at the same time as it is creating new transnational systems and forces. It is more than just the backdrop to contemporary policies: taken as a whole, globalization is transforming the institutions of the societies in which we live. It is certainly directly relevant to the rise of the 'new individualism' that has figured large in social democratic debates.

Five Dilemmas

Individualism

Solidarity has long been a theme of social democracy. The original legacy of Marxism was ambivalent on the theme of individualism versus collectivism. Marx spoke of the disappearance of the state with the coming of a fully mature socialist society, in which 'the free development of each will be the condition of the free development of all'. In practice, socialism and communism alike placed a firm emphasis upon the role of the state in generating both solidarity and equality. Collectivism became one of the most prominent traits distinguishing social democracy from conservatism, which ideologically placed a much stronger emphasis upon 'the individual'. A collectivist attitude has also long been part of Christian democratic ideology in Continental countries.

Much of this has been going into reverse since the late 1970s. Social democrats had to respond to the challenge of neoliberalism, but more important were the changes going on in Western countries that helped to give Thatcherism its ideological purchase. With some oversimplification, it could be said that classical social democracy was most successful and best developed in smaller countries, or countries with homogeneous national cultures. All Western countries, however, have become culturally more pluralistic, with a proliferation of lifestyles – a consequence, in some part, of the very affluence the 'welfare society' helped to produce.

Because their new stance is more based on a reluctant retreat from the old views than positively motiv-

34

ated, it isn't surprising that social democrats have struggled to accommodate to the rising importance of individualism and lifestyle diversity. They have been unable to make up their minds how far the new individualism is the same as the self-seeking individual portrayed in neoliberal economic theory, and hence to be hedged around with constraints. The idea of the 'autonomous individual', after all, was the very notion that socialism grew up in order to contest.

Several basic problems have to be confronted. What exactly is the new individualism? How does it relate to the expanding role now played by markets? Are we witnessing the rise of a 'me' generation, resulting in a 'me-first' society which inevitably destroys common values and public concerns? If personal liberty is to have greater emphasis from social democrats than in the past, how should the age-old problem of the relation between liberty and equality be tackled?

Left and right alike have been worried about the me-first society and its destructive consequences for social solidarity, but they trace it to different causes. Social democratic authors see its origins in market forces, together with the ideological impact of Thatcherism, with its stress that individuals should fend for themselves rather than depend on the state. The neoliberals and other conservatives look instead to the permissiveness of the 1960s, which set in train a process of moral decay.

Neither hypothesis stands up to close scrutiny. Research from different countries suggests that the whole debate needs to be recast. The 'me' generation is a misleading description of the new individualism, which does not signal a process of moral decay. Rather to the contrary, surveys show that younger generations today are sensitized to a greater range of moral concerns than previous generations were.[6] They do not, however, relate these values to tradition, or accept traditional forms of authority as legislating on questions of lifestyle. Some such moral values are clearly post-materialist in Inglehart's sense, concerning for example ecological values, human rights or sexual freedom.

As the sociologist Ulrich Beck observes, the new individualism:

> is *not* Thatcherism, not market individualism, not atomization. On the contrary, it means 'institutionalized individualism'. Most of the rights and entitlements of the welfare state, for example, are designed for individuals rather than for families. In many cases they presuppose employment. Employment in turn implies education and both of these presuppose mobility. By all these requirements people are invited to constitute themselves as individuals: to plan, understand, design themselves as individuals.[7]

The new individualism, in short, is associated with the retreat of tradition and custom from our lives, a phenomenon involved with the impact of globalization widely conceived rather than just the influence of markets. The welfare state has played its part: set up under the aegis of collectivism, welfare institutions have helped liberate individuals from some of the fixities of the past. Rather than seeing ours as an age of moral decay, then, it makes sense to see it as an age of moral transition. If institutional individualism is not the same as egoism, it poses less of a threat to social solidarity, but it does imply that we have to look for new means of producing that solidarity. Social cohesion can't be guaranteed by the top-down action of the state or by appeal to tradition. We have to make our lives in a more active way than was true of previous generations, and we need more actively to accept responsibilities for the consequences of what we do and the lifestyle habits we adopt. The theme of responsibility, or mutual obligation, was there in old-style social democracy, but was largely dormant, since it was sub merged within the concept of collective provision. We have to find a new balance between individual and collective responsibilities today.

Many leftish critics have a reserved attitude towards the new individualism. Self-fulfilment, the fulfilment of potential: aren't these just forms of therapy-talk, or the self-indulgence of the affluent? Obviously they may be, but to regard them as nothing more is to miss a sea change in people's attitudes and aspirations. The new individualism goes hand in hand with pressures towards greater democratization. All of us have to live in a more open and reflective manner than previous generations. This change is by no means only a beneficial one: new worries and anxieties come to the fore. But many more positive possibilities do too.

Left and right

Since its first beginnings, in the late eighteenth century, the distinction between left and right has remained ambiguous and difficult to pin down, yet obdurately refuses to disappear. In his history of political groups and parties that have described themselves as 'neither left nor right', the French historian of fascism Zeev Sternhell notes how contested the nature of the division has always been.[8] Left and right have also changed their meanings over time. A glance at the development of political thought shows that the same ideas have been regarded as left-wing in certain periods and contexts and right-wing in others. For example, advocates of free market philosophies were seen in the nineteenth century as on the left, but today are normally placed on the right. The claim that the left/right distinction is exhausted was made in the 1890s by syndicalists and advocates of 'solidarisme'. That claim has been repeated regularly across the years. Jean-Paul Sartre argued along these lines in the 1960s, but the thesis has been advanced as often by those coming from the right. In 1930, the historian Alain (Emile Chartier) observed: 'when I am asked whether the division between left and right still has any meaning, the first thought that comes to my mind is that the person who asks the question is not on the left'.[9]

The Italian political thinker Norberto Bobbio in 1994 published the most debated book on the theme of left and right in recent times.[10] The book was a bestseller on its original publication in Italy, selling over 200,000 copies in its first year. Bobbio sought to defend the continuing relevance of the distinction in the face of a spate of works declaring it to be obsolete – this time coming mainly from those with a background on the left rather than the right. Bobbio's arguments are worth listening to. The categories of left and right, he says, have continued to exert such an influence upon political thinking because politics is necessarily adversarial. The essence of politics is the struggle of opposing views and policies. Left and right come from the two sides of the body. Although what is 'on the left' or 'on the right' might change, nothing can be on the left and on the right at the same time. The distinction is a polarizing one.

When parties or political ideologies are more or less evenly balanced, Bobbio argues, few question the relevance of the distinction between left and right. But in times when one or the other becomes so strong that it seems 'the only game in town', both sides have interests in questioning that relevance. The side that is more powerful has an interest, as Margaret Thatcher proclaimed, in declaring that 'there is no alternative.' Since its ethos has become unpopular, the weaker side usually tries to take over some of the views of its opponents and propagate those as its own opinions. The classic strategy of the losing side is to produce a 'synthesis of opposing positions with the intention in practice of saving whatever can be saved of one's own position by drawing in the opposing position and thus neutralizing it'.[11] Each side represents itself as going beyond the old left/right distinction or combining elements of it to create a new and vital orientation.

The political right dressed itself up in new clothing, for example, in the period after World War II, following the fall of fascism. To survive, right-wing parties had to adopt some of the values of the left, and accept the basic framework of the welfare state. Since the early 1980s, things have been the other way around, because of the ideological ascendancy of neoliberalism and the collapse of communism. The claim that Tony Blair has taken over most of the views of Thatcherism and recycled them as something new is readily comprehensible from such a standpoint. This time it is the left that has most to gain from arguing that the old categories no longer make any sense. The distinction between left and right, according to Bobbio, will reassert itself, as it has done before. Thus, given that social democracy is reviving and the new right is rapidly becoming not so new, social democrats might soon stop hesitating about whether left and right are obsolete.

The left/right difference, in Bobbio's view, is not purely a matter of polarity. One major criterion continually reappears in distinguishing left from right: attitudes towards equality. The left favours greater equality, while the right sees society as inevitably hier-archical. Equality is a relative concept. We have to ask: equality between whom, of what, and in what degree? The left seeks to reduce inequality, but this goal can be understood in many different ways. It isn't the case that the left wishes to diminish all inequalities, while the right wants always to preserve them. The difference is contextual. For example, in a country having a recently arrived immigrant population, the contrast between left and right may be expressed in how far the immigrants should be accorded basic citizenship rights and material protection.

While arguing that the division between left and right will continue, Bobbio ends a 'Reply' to critics of

his book by accepting that the distinction hasn't now
got the purchase it used to have:

> It is undeniable that the reason for the current lack of
> direction in the left is that in the modern world prob-
> lems have emerged which the traditional movements of
> the left had never posed, and some of the assumptions
> on which they founded their strength and their plans
> for the transformation of society have not materialized
> . . . No left-winger can deny that the left today is not
> what it used to be.[12]

Bobbio is surely correct to say that the left/right distinction won't disappear, and to see inequality as at the
core of it. Although it can be interpreted in quite different ways, the idea of equality or social justice is basic
to the outlook of the left. It has been persistently
attacked by those on the right. Bobbio's definition,
however, needs some refining. Those on the left not
only pursue social justice, but believe that government
has to play a key role in furthering that aim. Rather
than speaking of social justice as such, it is more accur-
ate to say that to be on the left is to believe in a politics
of emancipation. Equality is important above all
because it is relevant to people's life chances, well-
being and self-esteem. As the Oxford philosopher
Joseph Raz puts it:

> what makes us care about various inequalities . . . is the
> hunger of the hungry, the need of the needy . . . the fact
> that they are worse off in the relevant respect than their
> neighbours is relevant. But it is relevant not as an inde-
> pendent evil of inequality. Its relevance is in showing
> that their hunger is greater, their need more pressing,

41

their suffering more hurtful and therefore it is our concern for equality that makes us give them priority.[13]

There are other reasons also to care about equality. A highly unequal society is harming itself by not making the best use of the talents and capacities of its citizens. Moreover, inequalities can threaten social cohesion and can have other socially undesirable consequences (such as provoking high rates of crime). It is true that there have been societies which have contained large inequalities and have none the less remained stable – the traditional Indian caste system, for example. In an age of mass democracy things are very different. A democratic society that generates large-scale inequality is likely to produce widespread disaffection and conflict.

Globalization together with the disintegration of communism have altered the contours of left and right. In the industrial countries there is no far left to speak of. But there is a far right, which increasingly defines itself in response to globalization – a common trend linking right-wing politicians such as Pat Buchanan in the US, Jean-Marie Le Pen in France and Pauline Hanson in Australia. The same is even true of the wilder fringes of the right, such as the Patriots in the US, who see the United Nations and the federal government alike as conspiracies against their national integrity. The themes of the far right are economic and cultural protectionism. Buchanan, for example, proclaims 'America first!' He defends national isolationism and a get-tough policy on immigration as the proper alternatives to 'globaloney'.

Five Dilemmas

The left/right distinction lives on, but a fundamental question for social democracy is whether the division covers as much of the political field as it used to do. Are we, as Bobbio seems to suggest, just in a period of transition, before left and right re-establish themselves with full force, or has there been a qualitative change in their relevance?

It would be difficult to resist the conclusion that there has been such a change. The reasons why have been well explored in the social democratic debates of the past few years. Whether or not they were directly influenced by Marxism, most thinkers and activists on the left took a progressivist view of history. They allied themselves closely not only with the 'forward march of socialism' but with the advance of science and technology. Conservatives, on the other hand, have been sceptical of grand schemes and pragmatic about social development, and have emphasized continuity. These contrasts today have become less sharp. Left and right alike have come to accept the double-edged nature of science and technology, which generate great benefits but also create new risks and uncertainties.

With the demise of socialism as a theory of economic management, one of the major division lines between left and right has disappeared, at least for the foreseeable future. The Marxist left wished to overthrow capitalism and replace it with a different system. Many social democrats also believed that capitalism could and should be progressively modified so that it would lose most of its defining characteristics. No one any longer has any alternatives to capitalism – the arguments that remain concern how far, and in what ways, capitalism should be governed and regulated. These arguments are certainly significant, but they fall short of the more fundamental disagreements of the past.

As these circumstances have shifted, a whole range of other problems and possibilities have come to the fore that are not within the reach of the left/right scheme. These include ecological questions, but also issues to do with the changing nature of family, work and personal and cultural identity. Of course, values of social justice and emancipation have a connection with all of these, but each of these issues cross-cuts those values. To the emancipatory politics of the classical left we have to add what I have elsewhere called life politics.[14] The term may or may not be a good one. What I mean by it is that, whereas emancipatory politics concerns life chances, life politics concerns life decisions. It is a politics of choice, identity and mutuality. How should we react to the hypothesis of global warming? Should we accept nuclear energy or not? How far should work remain a central life value? Should we favour devolution? What should be the future of the European Union? None of these is a clear left/right issue.

These considerations suggest that social democrats should take a new look at the political centre. Social democratic parties have moved towards the centre largely for opportunistic reasons. The political centre, of course, in the context of left and right can only mean compromise, the 'middle' between two more clear-cut alternatives. If left and right are less encompassing than they once were, however, this conclusion no longer follows. The idea of the 'active middle', or the 'radical centre', discussed quite widely among social democrats recently, should be taken seriously.

It implies that 'centre-left' isn't inevitably the same as 'moderate left'. Nearly all the questions of life politics mentioned above require radical solutions or suggest radical policies, on different levels of government. All are potentially divisive, but the conditions and alliances required to cope with them don't necessarily follow those based upon divisions of economic interest. In his *Culture of Contentment*, economist J.K. Galbraith suggested that in contemporary societies the affluent lose interest in the fate of the underprivileged.[15] Yet research in the European countries shows that in many respects the opposite is the case. Bottom-up alliances can be built, and can provide a basis for radical policies. Tackling ecological problems, for instance, certainly often demands a radical outlook, but that radicalism can in principle command widespread consensus. From responding to globalization to family policy the same applies.

The term 'centre-left' thus isn't an innocent label. A renewed social democracy has to be left of centre, because social justice and emancipatory politics remain at its core. But the 'centre' shouldn't be regarded as empty of substance. Rather, we are talking of the alliances that social democrats can weave from the threads of lifestyle diversity. Traditional as well as novel political problems need to be thought about in this way. A reformed welfare state, for example, has to meet criteria of social justice, but it has also to recognize and incorporate active lifestyle choice, be integrated with ecological strategies and respond to

45

new risk scenarios.

'Radicalism' used to be thought of as pitching left against right – and left against left, since self-proclaimed revolutionaries and Marxists saw themselves as quite distinct from those they regarded as mere 'reformers'. The equation between being on the left and being radical no longer stands up, if in fact it ever did. Many social democrats find such a situation uncomfortable, but it offers major gains, since it permits exchange across political fences that were once much higher. Consider again the example of welfare reform. There are big differences between social democrats and neoliberals about the future of the welfare state, and those differences cluster around the left/right division. Most social democrats want to keep welfare spending high, while neoliberals favour a more minimal welfare safety net. Yet there are also common issues faced by all welfare reformers. The question of how to deal with an ageing population, for instance, isn't just a matter of setting pension levels. It requires more radical rethinking in relation to the changing nature of ageing as such, changing patterns of health and disease, and more besides.

Political agency

In all attempts at political renewal the question of agency raises itself. If a coherent political programme can be assembled, how is it to be implemented? Social democratic parties originally began as social movements in the late nineteenth and early twentieth centuries. Today, in addition to undergoing their ideological crisis, they find themselves outflanked by new social movements and, like other parties, caught up in a situation where politics has become devalued and government apparently drained of power. Neoliberalism has mounted a sustained critique of the role of government in social and economic life, one that appears to resonate with trends in the real world. It is time for social democrats to launch a counterattack upon such views, which don't stand up when looked at closely.

The themes of the end of politics, and the swamping of the state by the global marketplace, have been so prominent in recent literature that it is worth reiterating what government can achieve in the contemporary world.

Government exists to:

- provide means for the representation of diverse interests;
- offer a forum for reconciling the competing claims of these interests;
- create and protect an open public sphere, in which unconstrained debate about policy issues can be carried on;
- provide a diversity of public goods, including forms of collective security and welfare;
- regulate markets in the public interest and foster market competition where monopoly threatens;
- foster social peace through control of the means of violence and through the provision of policing;
- promote the active development of human capital

through its core role in the education system;
- sustain an effective system of law;
- have a directly economic role, as a prime employer, in macro- and microeconomic intervention, plus the provision of infrastructure;
- more controversially, have a civilizing aim – government reflects widely held norms and values, but can also help shape them, in the educational system and elsewhere;
- foster regional and transnational alliances and pursue global goals.

Of course, these tasks can be interpreted in widely differing ways, and there are always areas of overlap with non-state agencies. The list is so formidable that to suppose that the state and government have become irrelevant makes no sense.

Markets cannot replace government in any of these areas, but neither can social movements or other kinds of non-governmental organization (NGO), no matter how significant they have become. Social movements and so-called 'challenger parties' haven't played as important a role in the UK in the 1980s and early 1990s as in many Continental countries. However, the changes produced by globalization have everywhere threatened to undermine orthodox political parties. Social democrats in the 1980s found themselves without an effective ideological framework with which to respond, while social movements and other groups pushed to the fore the issues that fell outside traditional social democratic politics – ecology, animal rights, sexuality, consumers' rights and many others.

What to some appeared as a process of depoliticization – the draining away of influence from national
governments and political parties – to others was a
spread of political engagement and activism. Ulrich
Beck speaks of the emergence of 'sub-politics' – politics
that has migrated away from parliament towards
single-issue groups in the society.[16] Many of these
groups, such as Greenpeace or Oxfam, operate on a
global scale. A key episode for Beck and many others
was that of Brent Spar. The Shell oil company planned
in 1995 to dispose of the Brent Spar oil rig by sinking
it to the ocean bed. Environmental groups mounted
vigorous protests and consumers in many countries
stopped buying Shell petrol. The changes in attitude in
the company since that time have been far-reaching.

In 1998 Shell published a substantial report describing its new attitudes towards corporate responsibility.
The report speaks of engaging in a 'global debate', 'in
order to learn from others' and 'explain our actions'. It
accepts that there is a 'responsibility to ensure that our
businesses are run in a way that is ethically acceptable
to the rest of the world' and that 'we must show we are
doing so by providing independently verified assur-
ance'. Shell claims to be the first major energy company
publicly to support the UN Universal Declaration of
Human Rights. A Social Responsibility Committee was
set up in 1997 to review the policies and conduct of
Shell businesses.[17]

A speech made by Cor Herkstroter, the world chair-
man of Shell, is revealing. Of environmental and con-
sumer groups he says, 'we were somewhat slow in
understanding that these groups were tending to

acquire authority. We underestimated the extent of these changes – we failed to engage in a serious dialogue with these new groups.' He adds, 'simply put, the institutions of global society are being reinvented as technology redefines relationships between individuals and organizations'.

The new movements, groups and NGOs thus are able to flex their muscles on the world scene and even global corporations have to take notice. Beck compares 'the immobility of the government apparatus' with the 'mobility of agents on all possible levels of society' and 'the petering out of politics' with 'the activation of sub-politics'. Citizens' initiative groups, he argues, have taken power unilaterally, without waiting for the politicians. They, not the politicians, have put ecological issues, and many other new concerns too, on the agenda. Citizens' groups brought about the transitions in Eastern Europe in 1989: 'with no copying machines or telephones', they 'were able to force the ruling groups to retreat and collapse just by assembling in a square'.[18]

The cultural critic Hans Magnus Enzensberger writes of Germany – and by implication of other countries too:

> The politicians are insulted that people are less and less interested in them . . . [but] innovations and decisions on the future have not originated from the political class for some time now. . . . The [German] Federal Government is relatively stable and relatively successful, despite and not because of the fact that it is ruled by those people grinning down at us from the campaign posters. . . . Germany can afford an incompetent

government, because ultimately the people who bore us
in the daily news really do not matter.[19]

Such comments are consistent with research findings
about declining trust in politicians and the machinery
of orthodox politics, similar in most industrial countries. In the US, 76 per cent of people in an opinion
poll in 1964 answered 'all' or 'most of the time' when
asked 'How much of the time do you trust the government in Washington to do the right thing?' A repeat
poll in 1994 showed the proportion had dropped to 25
per cent. Of those expressing continuing trust in
government, 61 per cent voted in the previous presi-
dential elections, compared with 35 per cent of the less
trustful. Younger people have a more reserved attitude
to parliamentary politics than older generations have,
although the young have a greater interest than their
elders in issues of 'sub-politics'. The 'long civic generation' born between 1910 and 1940 is most likely to
trust in politicians and to vote.[20] A poll taken in eleven
West European countries in 1981 and repeated in 1990
showed confidence in government institutions had
declined in six countries, was stable but quite low in
four and had risen only in one (Denmark). It isn't just
that people express less confidence in politicians than
they used to: the same is true of their attitudes to other
authority figures, such as the police, lawyers or
doctors.[21]

'Challenger parties' have sought to exploit these sen-
timents by attacking the orthodox parties directly.
Green parties and far right populist parties have
challenged for a share of power in most industrial

countries. Both types of party are linked to wider social movements and both explicitly protest against established parties and systems of government. As of 1998, greens have deputies in eleven national parliaments in Europe. The right-wing populist parties, which were mostly set up in the 1980s, have a more varied representation, with up to 20 per cent support in some countries, as the Freiheitliche Partei has in Austria, and virtually no presence at all in others, such as the UK, Spain, Holland or Norway.

There is no sign that these parties will gain more electoral support than they have achieved so far, although this sometimes puts them in the position of power brokers. Like social movements and activist groups, their importance is largely symbolic: they push issues onto the political agenda, and give concrete form to the struggles that surround them. Far right parties and movements would be dangerous if they did become anything more than minority concerns. The greens, on the other hand, pose ideological questions that are impossible to ignore, and that place in question some of the basic orientations of social democracy. In spite of the ten-year-old discussions of 'ecological modernization' it cannot be said that social democrats have been able adequately to assimilate ecological thinking. 'Even in opposition, the established left in most countries had not convincingly demonstrated by the late 1990s that they had changed their stand with respect to the new issues.'[22] Partly the difficulty is that the intellectual and policy problems involved are formidable. Also most social democratic parties are split, a consequence of being in a halfway house where old left ideas remain prominent and no fully fledged alternative has been formed.

How far will 'sub-politics' replace the more conventional spheres of politics and government? Beck is right to argue that declining interest in party and parliamentary politics isn't the same as depoliticization. Social movements, single-issue groups, NGOs and other associations of citizens surely will play a part in politics on a continuing basis – from a local through to a world level. Governments will have to be ready to learn from them, react to the issues they raise and negotiate with them, as will corporations and other business agencies.

Yet the idea that such groups can take over where government is failing, or can stand in place of political parties, is fantasy. The nation-state and national government may be changing their form, but both retain a decisive importance in the present-day world. The 'people who bore us in the daily news' do matter, and will do so for the indefinite future. The 1989 changes in Eastern Europe in fact depended at least upon the connivance of states and states' leaders – particularly the decision of the Soviet leadership not to send in troops to quell the demonstrations. However significant movements and special-interest groups may be, they cannot as such govern. One of the main functions of government is precisely to reconcile the divergent claims of special-interest groups, in practice and in law. But 'government' here should be understood in a more general sense than only national government. Social democrats have to consider how government might best be reconstructed to meet the needs of the age.

Ecological issues

The importance of ecological politics goes far beyond whatever influence green social movements might muster, or the proportion of the vote green parties might achieve. In concrete politics the influence of ecological groups has already been considerable, especially in Germany – it isn't surprising that the notion of 'subpolitics' originated there. In their work *The German Left*, Andrei Markovits and Philip Gorski observe that 'throughout the 1980s the greens developed into the German left's socializing agent in the sense that virtually all its new ideas, political innovations, strategic formulations, lifestyle . . . originated from the greens and their milieu'.[23] Chancellor Willy Brandt was fond of saying the greens were the 'lost children of the SPD', but in truth the social democrats were revitalized by their enforced confrontation with the ecological movement. The consequences are tangible. Germany is one of the leading countries in the world in terms of environmental measures such as energy efficiency (amount of energy needed to produce a unit of national income) or per capita emissions of pollutants like carbon dioxide or sulphur dioxide.

Environmental movements, of course, are not cut out of whole cloth, and the ecological field is rife with controversies. Premonitions of possible global catastrophe were first expressed in the 1960s and soon blossomed into full-blown predictions. The earth's resources, it was proclaimed, are being consumed at a frightening rate, while pollution is destroying the ecological balance upon which the continuity of nature depends.

These dire warnings provoked a robust response from critics, who argued that indefinite economic growth is possible. They did so mainly on the basis of neoliberal economic theory. Market principles will ensure that there are no limits to growth. Like other goods, if any natural resource becomes scarcer its price will rise and its consumption will fall. If the price of goods goes down, it means that supply is outpacing demand. The economist Julian Simon struck a famous wager with environmentalist Paul Ehrlich in 1980. Simon bet that, for any set of natural resources Ehrlich might like to nominate, prices would be lower at a specified moment in the future. Ehrlich chose 1990, and selected copper, chrome, nickel, tin and tungsten. By 1990 the prices of these materials were lower by from 24 per cent to 78 per cent than they had been ten years before. Ehrlich duly paid up.

So far as pollution is concerned, Simon and others who argue along similar lines simply tend to deny that there is any cause for worry. Global warming, for example, either is not happening, or is a natural phenomenon rather than brought about by human activities. Nature has restorative properties that go well beyond any impact human beings might have on the environment – for instance, nature is always creating new species as well as destroying them.[24]

Is such a view defensible? I don't believe so. Market solutions are possible for a diversity of ecological problems, yet as elsewhere this shouldn't imply opting for market fundamentalism. To be sanguine about environmental dangers would itself be a highly dangerous strategy. Recognizing this fact means engaging with the ideas of sustainable development and ecological modernization, as most social democratic parties have rightly recognized.

Since its inclusion in the Brundtland Commission report in 1987, sustainable development has become the dominant concern of environmental groups, and politicians of most persuasions pay at least lip service to it. Brundtland provided a deceptively simple definition of sustainable development, as the capability of the current generation 'to ensure that it meets the needs of the present without compromising the ability of future generations to meet their own needs'.[25] Since we don't know what the needs of future generations will be, or how resource utilization will be affected by technological change, the notion of sustainable development doesn't admit of precision – it isn't surprising that as many as forty different definitions of it have been counted.

Sustainable development thus is more of a guiding principle than a precise formula. Nevertheless, it was endorsed in Agenda 21, a programme sponsored by the UN as a detailed follow-up to Brundtland's efforts. Several countries have made major efforts to build it into their economic thinking. Amazingly, the conservative government in the UK in 1988 claimed that British economic policy complied with the principles of sustainable development, showing how pliant the concept is.

Britain's attitude in the late 1980s and early 1990s contrasted markedly with that of some Continental countries – for instance Holland, which in 1989 set up a national plan to integrate ecological criteria into the routine workings of all government departments. Each department has environmental quality targets and a set timetable within which to achieve them. Sustainable development is defined as the avoidance of 'end-of-pipe' technologies in favour of modes of production that are designed from the beginning to avoid or limit pollution. Citizens' groups and industry representatives take part in the meetings leading up to the planning of targets. The scheme has had the usual share of setbacks and difficulties, but has played its part in making Holland a country with one of the best environmental records.

The notion of sustainable development fits well with the broader one of ecological modernization. Maarten Hajer, one of its leading theorists, sees ecological modernization as pulling together several 'credible and attractive story-lines': sustainable development in place of 'defining growth'; a preference for anticipation rather than cure; equating pollution with inefficiency; and treating environmental regulation and economic growth as mutually beneficial.[26] While government intervention is necessary to promote sound environmental principles, it involves the active cooperation of industry – hopefully, its willing cooperation, via the recognition that ecological modernization is beneficial for business. 'Ecological modernization implies a partnership in which governments, businesses, moderate environmentalists, and scientists cooperate in the restructuring of the capitalist political economy along more environmentally defensible lines.'[27]

Too good to be true? It is. There is no doubt that ecological modernization links social democratic and ecological concerns more closely than once seemed possible. It has real achievements to its name: countries most influenced by the idea of ecological modernization are the cleanest and greenest of the industrial nations. Yet, claiming to get the best of all worlds, ecological modernization skirts some of the main challenges ecological problems pose for social democratic thought. It isn't really convincing to suppose that environmental protection and economic development fit together comfortably – the one is bound sometimes to come into conflict with the other. Moreover, ecological modernization is largely a matter of national policy, but environmental hazards mostly cut across the borders of nations and some are global in scope.

The somewhat comfortable assumptions of ecological modernization deflect attention from two fundamental questions raised by ecological considerations: our relationship to scientific advance, and our response to risk. Partly as a consequence of globalization, scientific and technological change has speeded up, and its influence upon our lives has become both more immediate and profound. We might think of 'the environment' as the natural world, but of course it isn't that any longer. Much of what used to be natural is now either the product of, or influenced by, human activity – not just the external world, including possibly the earth's climate, but the 'internal environment' of the body. For better or for worse, science and technology have invaded the human body, and have redrawn the boundary between what can be humanly achieved and what we simply have to 'accept' from nature.

Science and technology used to be seen as outside politics, but this view has become obsolete. All of us live in a more 'interrogatory' relationship with science and industrial innovation than used to be the case. 'New expressways, rubbish incinerator plants, chemical, nuclear or biotechnical factories and research institutes encounter the resistance of the immediately affected population groups. That, and not (as in early industrialization) rejoicing at this progress, is what has come to be predictable.'[28] Decision-making in these contexts cannot be left to the 'experts', but has to involve politicians and citizens. In short, science and technology cannot stay outside democratic processes. Experts cannot be relied upon automatically to know what is good for us, nor can they always provide us with unambiguous truths; they should be called upon to justify their conclusions and policies in the face of public scrutiny.

The BSE crisis in the UK is seen by many as a one-off – as a British problem, or in the eyes of some on the left as a Thatcherite failure of regulation. It isn't either, or it isn't only these. The BSE episode should rather be understood as typical of risk situations that develop when 'nature is no longer nature'. Characteristic of the new risk situations is that the experts disagree with each other. Rather than there being a clear-cut set of findings to turn to for policy-makers, research generates ambiguous conclusions and disputed interpretations.

With many standard risks, trends are historically established. Risks can be calculated on the basis of past experience. The risk of a driver being involved in a traffic accident over a given period of time can easily be calculated on a statistical basis. The new risk situations aren't like this. We don't have past experience to guide us, and even whether there are any risks at all may be vociferously argued over. The majority of scientists in the field believe that global warming is occurring, that it has human causes, and that it holds possible disasters in store for humanity. However, a significant minority of specialists believe none of these things and, as we have seen, some contributors to the environmental literature agree.

The BSE events as yet are far from played out. No one knows how many other countries BSE may appear in, or what its longer-term consequences might be. The precise mode of its transmission across species is a mystery and it may have a long gestation period. Its purely economic impact has already been considerable. The latest estimate from the BSE enquiry in 1998 puts its cost to the UK economy so far at £3 billion, measured only in terms of compensation paid to farmers and the costs of destroying infected cattle and disposing of their remains. Beef consumption has fallen in a number of countries as yet unaffected in a direct way by BSE.

The BSE episode gives ample evidence, if evidence were needed, that ecological risks can't be 'kept on one side', but flood into the core areas of modern politics. It is obvious, for instance, that health-care policies can't be designed as though controlling pollution were a distinct area of 'the environment', or as though they were separate from processes of technological change. Coping with ecological risk will be a problematic affair for the foreseeable future.

Five Dilemmas

In the literature of ecological modernization, the precautionary principle is usually offered as a means of dealing with ecological threats. The concept seems first to have been used in Germany in the 1980s, and has to some extent formed part of public policy in that country. At its simplest, it states that action on environmental issues should be taken even though there is scientific uncertainty about them. Thus in several Continental countries programmes were initiated to counter acid rain in the 1980s, whereas in Britain lack of conclusive evidence was used to justify inactivity on this and other pollution problems too.

Yet the precautionary principle isn't always helpful or even applicable. Ecological risk often won't be normalized in this way, because in many situations we no longer have the option of 'staying close to nature', or because the balance of benefits and dangers from scientific and technological advance is imponderable. We may need quite often to be bold rather than cautious in supporting scientific and technological innovation.

The complex character of the new risk situations extends even to the manner in which they enter into public debate. Take the example of BSE again. The government of the time has been widely blamed for first of all denying that BSE poses a health risk to humans, then later reversing its stance in the light of new scientific evidence. It is all too easy to dismiss such inconsistency as government incompetence. Where new risks exist, and scientific evidence is incomplete, governments must take decisions that are by definition a leap in the dark. An elemental uncertainty is involved in when and how to announce possible dangers that

61

have come to light via new scientific information. Public announcement of a new risk scenario, as the BSE episode shows, can have profound consequences. If a risk is publicized – or given 'official' status by the intervention of government – and turns out to have been exaggerated or non-existent, critics will say 'scare-mongering'. Suppose, however, the authorities either believe the risk is low, or are cautious about making an announcement. The critics will say 'cover-up' – why wasn't the public informed earlier?

The problems involved here are even more difficult than this. Sometimes scaring people might be necessary in order to persuade them either to alter their behaviour, or to accept the steps that should be taken to avoid a particular danger or set of dangers. Effective world action to counter global warming, for example, is only likely to be initiated if governments and other agencies become significantly disturbed about the disasters that might otherwise ensue. Yet there is presumably a limit to the number of scares that can or should be publicly promoted. If there are too many, there is the chance that none will be taken seriously.

Providing citizens with security has long been a concern of social democrats. The welfare state has been seen as the vehicle of such security. One of the main lessons to be drawn from ecological questions is that just as much attention needs to be given to risk. The new prominence of risk connects individual autonomy on the one hand with the sweeping influence of scientific and technological change on the other. Risk draws attention to the dangers we face – the most important of which we have created for ourselves – but also to the opportunities that go along with them. Risk is not just a negative phenomenon – something to be avoided or minimized. It is at the same time the energizing principle of a society that has broken away from tradition and nature.

Tradition and nature are alike in the sense that they take many decisions 'out of play'. Activities and events are 'always done this way' or are accepted as 'natural'. Once tradition and nature are transformed, forward-looking decisions have to be taken, and we have responsibility for their consequences. Who should bear responsibility for the future consequences of present activities (whether of individuals, nations or other groups) is one of the major concerns of the new politics, as is who provides security if things go wrong, how and with what resources.

The risk matrix

Opportunity	Innovation
Security	Responsibility

Opportunity and innovation are the positive side of risk. No one can escape risk, of course, but there is a basic difference between the passive experience of risk and the active exploration of risk environments. A positive engagement with risk is a necessary component of social and economic mobilization. Some risks we wish to minimize as far as possible; others, such as those involved in investment decisions, are a positive and inevitable part of a successful market economy.

Risk isn't exactly the same as danger. Risk refers to dangers we seek actively to confront and assess. In a society such as ours, oriented towards the future and saturated with information, the theme of risk unites many otherwise disparate areas of politics: welfare state reform, engagement with world financial markets, responses to technological change, ecological problems and geopolitical transformations. We all need protection against risk, but also the capability to confront and take risks in a productive fashion.

Third way politics

So far I have discussed the 'five dilemmas' separately, as though they were independent of one another. Of course, they aren't, and in this and subsequent chapters we need to tie the threads together.

The overall aim of third way politics should be to help citizens pilot their way through the major revolutions of our time: *globalization, transformations in personal life* and our *relationship to nature*. Third way politics should take a positive attitude towards globalization – but, crucially, only as a phenomenon ranging much more widely than the global marketplace. Social democrats need to contest economic and cultural protectionism, the territory of the far right, which sees globalization as a threat to national integrity and traditional values. Economic globalization plainly can have destructive effects upon local self-sufficiency. Yet protectionism is neither sensible nor desirable. Even if it could be made to work, it would create a world of selfish and probably warring economic blocs. Third way politics should not identify globalization with a blanket endorsement of free trade. Free trade can be an engine of economic development, but given the socially and culturally destructive power of markets, its wider consequences need always to be scrutinized.

Third way politics should preserve a core concern with social justice, while accepting that the range of questions which escape the left/right divide is greater than before. Equality and individual freedom may conflict, but egalitarian measures also often increase the range of freedoms open to individuals. Freedom to social democrats should mean autonomy of action, which in turn demands the involvement of the wider social community. Having abandoned collectivism, third way politics looks for a new relationship between the individual and the community, a redefinition of rights and obligations.

One might suggest as a prime motto for the new politics, *no rights without responsibilities*. Government has a whole cluster of responsibilities for its citizens and others, including the protection of the vulnerable. Old-style social democracy, however, was inclined to treat rights as unconditional claims. With expanding individualism should come an extension of individual obligations. Unemployment benefits, for example, should carry the obligation to look actively for work, and it is up to governments to ensure that welfare systems do not discourage active search. As an ethical principle, 'no rights without responsibilities' must apply not only to welfare recipients, but to everyone. It is highly important for social democrats to stress this, because otherwise the precept can be held to apply only to the poor or to the needy – as tends to be the case with the political right.

A second precept, in today's society, should be *no authority without democracy*. The right has always looked to traditional symbols as the prime means of justifying authority, whether in the nation, government, the family or other institutions.[29] Right-wing thinkers and politicians argue that without tradition, and traditional forms of deference, authority crumbles – people lose the ability to differentiate between right and wrong. Consequently democracy can never be more than partial. Social democrats should oppose this view. In a society where tradition and custom are losing their hold, the only route to the establishing of authority is via democracy. The new individualism doesn't inevitably corrode authority, but demands it be recast on an active or participatory basis.

Third way values

Equality
Protection of the vulnerable
Freedom as autonomy
No rights without responsibilities
No authority without democracy
Cosmopolitan pluralism
Philosophic conservatism

Other issues with which third way politics is concerned do not belong to the framework of emancipatory politics, or only partially concern such a framework. They include responses to globalization, scientific and technological change, and our relationship to the natural world. The questions to be asked here are not about social justice, but about how we should live after the decline of tradition and custom, how to recreate social solidarity and how to react to ecological problems. In response to these questions, strong emphasis has to be given to cosmopolitan values, and to what might be called philosophic conservatism. In an era of ecological risk, modernization cannot be purely linear and certainly cannot be simply equated with economic growth.

The issue of modernization is a basic one for the new politics. Ecological modernization is one version, but there are others too. Tony Blair's speeches, for example, are peppered with talk of modernization. What should modernization be taken to mean? One thing it means, obviously, is the modernizing of social democracy itself – the breaking away from classical social democratic positions. As an agenda of a wider kind, however, a modernizing strategy can work only if social democrats have a sophisticated understanding of the concept.

Modernization that is ecologically sensitive is not about 'more and more modernity', but is conscious of the problems and limitations of modernizing processes. It is alive to the need to re-establish continuity and develop social cohesion in a world of erratic transformation, where the intrinsically unpredictable energies of scientific and technological innovation play such an important role.

The theme of philosophic conservatism is central. Modernization and conservatism, of course, are normally treated as opposites. However, we must use the tools of modernity to cope with living in a world 'beyond tradition' and 'on the other side of nature', where risk and responsibility have a new mix.

'Conservatism' in this sense has only a loose affinity with the way it has been understood on the political right. It suggests a pragmatic attitude towards coping with change; a nuanced view of science and technology, in recognition of their ambiguous consequences for us; a respect for the past and for history; and in the environmental arena, an adoption of the precautionary principle where feasible. These goals are not only not incompatible with a modernizing agenda; they presuppose it. Science and technology, as discussed above, can no longer be left outside the scope of democracy, since they influence our lives in a more direct and far-reaching way than was true for previous generations.

As another example, take the family, which figures in some of the most contentious debates in modern politics. Sustaining continuity in family life, especially protecting the well-being of children, is one of the most important goals of family policy. This can't be achieved, however, through a reactionary stance, an attempt to reinstate the 'traditional family'. As I shall try to show below, it presumes a modernizing agenda of democratization.

3

State and Civil Society

The ideas developed in what follows offer the outline – and it is no more than an outline – of an integrated political programme, covering each of the major sectors of society. Reform of the state and government should be a basic orienting principle of third way politics – a process of the deepening and widening of democracy. Government can act in partnership with agencies in civil society to foster community renewal and development. The economic basis of such partnership is what I shall call the new mixed economy. That economy can be effective only if existing welfare institutions are thoroughly modernized. Third way politics is one-nation politics. The cosmopolitan nation helps promote social inclusion but also has a key role in fostering transnational systems of governance.

Each of these concepts will be discussed in some detail in the subsequent sections. I don't want to suggest any of the notions I shall propose are unproblematic. On the contrary, almost all are debatable and difficult. We don't know if we will be able adequately

to control the forces that globalization and technological change have unleashed. The new risk environments have an enigmatic mixture of dangers and
advantages. The framework suggested here thus represents a programme in the making.

The third way programme

The radical centre
The new democratic state (the state without
    enemies)
Active civil society
The democratic family
The new mixed economy
Equality as inclusion
Positive welfare
The social investment state
The cosmopolitan nation
Cosmopolitan democracy

Democratizing democracy

The neoliberals want to shrink the state; the social
democrats, historically, have been keen to expand it.
The third way argues that what is necessary is to reconstruct it – to go beyond those on the right 'who say
government is the enemy', and those on the left 'who
say government is the answer'.

If there is a crisis of liberal democracy today, it is
not, as half a century ago, because it is threatened by
hostile rivals, but on the contrary because it has no

70

rivals. With the passing of the bipolar era, most states have no clear-cut enemies. States facing dangers rather than enemies have to look for sources of legitimacy different from those in the past. The modern state was forged in the crucible of war, and war or preparing for it influenced most aspects of state institutions. Citizenship rights and welfare programmes were mainly established as states sought to engage their populations and hold their support, a phenomenon that continued through the Cold War period. This fact has been ignored by many social democratic authors – including perhaps the most influential, T.H. Marshall – who see the development of liberal democracy and the welfare state as more self-contained processes than they actually were.

The advance of the global marketplace and the retreat of large-scale war are not the only factors affecting the structure of states or the legitimacy of governments. Other influences include the very spread of democratization, which is closely connected with the lapsing influence of tradition and custom. The appeal of democracy does not come wholly, or perhaps even primarily, from the triumph of liberal democratic institutions over others, but from the deeper forces that are reshaping the global society, including the demand for individual autonomy and the emergence of a more reflexive citizenry. Democratization is outflanking democracy, and the imbalance must be addressed.

The crisis of democracy comes from its not being democratic enough. While, as discussed in the previous chapter, the proportion of people expressing trust in politicians has dipped over the past three decades, faith in democracy as such has not. Of the population in the US, 90 per cent are 'satisfied with a democratic form of government.'[1] A survey of eleven European countries covering the period 1981–90 also showed that over 90 per cent approved of 'the democratic system of government'. The same proportion agreed that 'we should look for ways to develop democracy further'.

The issue isn't more government or less, but recognizing that governance must adjust to the new circumstances of the global age; and that authority, including state legitimacy, has to be renewed on an active basis. In a post-traditional society, authority can no longer be legitimated by traditional symbols or by saying 'This is how things have always been done.' What reforms should be pushed for? How can we democratize democracy? The answers depend partly on context, since different countries have followed different trajectories, and have varying constitutional backgrounds. But the overall emphases should be the same everywhere. They can be summarized in the following way:

(1) The state must respond structurally to globalization. The democratizing of democracy first of all implies decentralization – but not as a one-way process. Globalization creates a strong impetus and logic to the downward devolution of power, but also to upward devolution. Rather than merely weakening the authority of the nation-state, this double movement – a movement of double democratization – is the condition of reasserting that authority, since this movement can make the state more responsive to the influences that otherwise outflank it all round. In the

context of the European Union, this means treating subsidiarity as more than a doctrinal term: it is the way to construct a political order which is neither a super-state nor only a free trade area, and at the same time clothes the nation with renewed influence.

(2) The state should expand the role of the public sphere, which means constitutional reform directed towards greater transparency and openness, as well as the intro-duction of new safeguards against corruption. It isn't by chance that governments all round the world have faced accusations of corruption in recent years. The reason isn't that corruption is on the increase, but that the nature of the political environment has changed. Supposedly quite open, liberal democratic institutions in most countries have in practice depended upon backstage deals, privilege and patronage. One of the biggest changes affecting the political sphere is that governments and citizens increas-ingly now live in a single information environment. Exist-ing ways of doing things come under scrutiny and the scope of what is seen as corrupt or unacceptable widens.

One of the specific difficulties – or is it an opportun-ity? – for the UK is that the country needs a two-fold process of constitutional modernization. Constitutional reform of a broad kind has been on the agenda since Charter 88 placed it there ten years ago, and has become part of Labour's policy agenda. When first mooted, such reform was inspired by the idea that Britain needed to catch up with more advanced consti-tutional models elsewhere. Now it needs in addition to react to more encompassing trends.

Unlike virtually all other liberal democracies, Britain

has no written constitution. Only in custom and to some extent in case law are the functions of government and the rights and duties of citizens set out. Constitutional change should aim not only to make these principles explicit, but to combat the culture of secrecy that has pervaded the higher levels of British institutions. The executive holds too much power and the existing forms of accountability are weak; parliamentary committees reflect the composition of the Commons and rarely have much bite. As it stands, the House of Lords is an anachronism in a democratic society.

At first sight, reform in any one of those areas looks formidably difficult, let alone in all taken together. After all, reform has to take place through the very institutions that are the problem. Yet Labour in power has already made a bold start, and it is just possible that what seem deeply entrenched ways of doing things might prove open to change when actively confronted.

(3) To retain or regain legitimacy, states without enemies have to elevate their administrative efficiency. Government at all levels is mistrusted partly because it is cumbersome and ineffective. In a world where business organizations respond rapidly to change and are more agile on their feet, government can lag behind. After all, the term 'bureaucracy', with its attendant connotations of red tape, was invented to refer to government. The restructuring of government should follow the ecological principle of 'getting more from less', understood not as downsizing but as improving delivered value. Most governments still have a good deal to learn from business best practice – for instance, target controls, effective

auditing, flexible decision structures and increased employee participation – the last of these being a factor in democratization. Social democrats must respond to the criticism that, lacking market discipline, state institutions become lazy and the services they deliver shoddy.

As the American political commentator E.J. Dionne points out, the argument can become a parody of itself, as if government were synonymous with inefficiency, ignoring the existence of fine schools, public hospitals or parks.[2] The appropriate response is not to introduce market mechanisms, or quasi-markets, wherever there is the glimmer of a possibility. The idea that government should mimic the marketplace was the main thrust of David Osborne and Ted Gaebler's book *Reinventing Government*.[3] Their work influenced Clinton's policies in the early 1990s. Reinventing government certainly sometimes means adopting market-based solutions. But it also should mean reasserting the effectiveness of government in the face of markets.

(4) The downward pressure of globalization introduces not only the possibility but the necessity of forms of democracy other than the orthodox voting process. Government can re-establish more direct contact with citizens, and citizens with government, through 'experiments with democracy' – local direct democracy, electronic referenda, citizens' juries and other possibilities. These won't substitute for normal voting mechanisms in local and central government, but could become an enduring complement to them. One model is the approach used in Sweden twenty years ago, when the government drew the public directly into the

formulation of energy policy. The government, unions, parties and education agencies set up day-long courses on energy. Anyone who took such a course could make formal recommendations to the government. Seventy thousand people participated in an exercise that decisively shaped policy.

(5) States without enemies depend for their legitimacy more than before upon their capacity for risk management. The management of risk, as was stressed earlier, doesn't concern only the provision of security, which is the way risk has ordinarily been understood in the context of the welfare state. Nor does it concern only economic risks: other risks, coming for instance from science and technology, also impinge directly upon government. Government is necessarily and intrinsically in the business of regulating scientific and technological change, as well as dealing with the ethical questions it raises.

Characterizing risk, as discussed earlier, cannot just be left to experts. From the beginning it demands public involvement. Among the many different situations that can arise are those where the hazard is serious but trust in the responsible organization is low. Deliberative procedures are needed at each step leading to risk decisions and normally should involve experts, government and lay individuals. The object of risk characterization is to illuminate practical choices and the limits of available scientific or technical knowledge. The complex nature of many risk situations means that the framework for debate often needs to be large.

The California Comparative Risk Project is an instructive example of how risk assessment and deliberative citizen involvement can be combined. Three technical committees were set up on health, ecological protection and social welfare, to work independently to rank risks in their categories. Three other committees were established to consider how risks might be managed and their legal and economic implications. The two sets of committees were then brought together and asked to reach conclusions. The lay committees raised many concerns that the technical ones simply ignored, leading to a rich public debate about risk criteria, some of which later fed into public policy.

(6) The democratizing of democracy cannot be only local or national – the state must have a cosmopolitan outlook, while upward democratization should not stop at the regional level. Downward democratization presumes the renewal of civil society, of which more later. These points taken together define a form of government which it should be the aim of social democrats to promote: the new democratic state.

The new democratic state (the state without enemies)

Devolution
Double democratization
Renewal of the public sphere – transparency
Administrative efficiency
Mechanisms of direct democracy
Government as risk manager

The new democratic state is an ideal, and something of an open-ended one at that. I don't pretend to unpack any of the detail that would be needed to give it real flesh. Moreover, all reforms bring their own complexities. Decentralization and devolution, for example, have an attractive ring to them – return power to the regions, the cities, the neighbourhoods! Like all democratizing processes their benefits come with strings attached. Devolution can lead to fragmentation if not balanced with a transfer of power 'upwards'. It is not intrinsically democratizing: it has to be made so. As critics point out, devolution can add layers of local bureaucratic power to those that already exist at the political centre. Britain's 'poor, sad cities', it has been said, could be regenerated through greater self-government, and this is surely true.[4] Among the obvious dangers, however, is that some cities or regions could thereby forge ahead of others, worsening the marked regional inequalities that already exist in the UK.

The question of civil society

The fostering of an active civil society is a basic part of the politics of the third way. In contrast to the old left, which tended to be dismissive of worries about civic decline, the new politics accepts that such anxieties are genuine. Civic decline is real and visible in many sectors of contemporary societies, not just an invention of conservative politicians. It is seen in the weakening sense of solidarity in some local communities and urban neighbourhoods, high levels of crime, and the break-up of marriages and families.

The right tends to deny that economic deprivation is associated with these problems. But it is just as wrong to reduce civic decline to economics, as the old left often did, as to deny the influence of poverty and underprivilege. We can't blame the erosion of civility on the welfare state, or suppose that it can be reversed by leaving civil society to its own devices. Government can and must play a major part in renewing civic culture.

The renewal of civil society

Government and civil society in partnership
Community renewal through harnessing local
  initiative
Involvement of the third sector
Protection of the local public sphere
Community-based crime prevention
The democratic family

State and civil society should act in partnership, each to facilitate, but also to act as a control upon, the other. The theme of community is fundamental to the new politics, but not just as an abstract slogan. The advance of globalization makes a community focus both necessary and possible, because of the downward pressure it exerts. 'Community' doesn't imply trying to recapture lost forms of local solidarity; it refers to practical means of furthering the social and material refurbishment of neighbourhoods, towns and larger local areas. There are no permanent boundaries between government and civil society. Depending on context, government needs sometimes to be drawn further into the civil arena, sometimes to retreat. Where government withdraws from direct involvement, its resources might still be necessary to support activities that local groups take over or introduce – above all in poorer areas. Yet it is particularly in poorer communities that the fostering of local initiative and involvement can generate the highest return.

Diminished trust in politicians and other authority figures is sometimes taken to indicate general social apathy. As mentioned, it does not – perhaps the opposite. An increasingly reflexive society is also one marked by high levels of self-organization. Research in the US, the UK and elsewhere tends to indicate a burgeoning civil sphere, at least in some areas and contexts. Some older forms of civil association and civic engagement are losing their purchase, but other sorts of communal energy are replacing them. The point is to harness these to wider social ends in ways that benefit local communities as well as the society as a whole.

Robert Wuthnow has studied the development of the small-group movement in the US. By small groups, he means small numbers of people who meet together in a regular way to develop their common interests. On the basis of extensive research, he concludes that 40 per cent of Americans – some 75 million – belong to at least one small group that meets regularly. In such groups a feeling of community is generated, but not only in the old sense of being part of a local area. Rather, people with similar concerns get together to pursue a 'journey through life':

Small groups are doing a better job than many of their critics would like to think. The communities they create are seldom frail. People feel cared for. They help one another . . . The attachments that develop among the members of small groups demonstrate clearly that we are not a society of rugged individualists who wish to go it entirely alone but, rather, that . . . even amidst the dislocating tendencies of our society, we are capable of banding together in bonds of mutual support.[5]

Many of the groups originated in the 1960s, and reflect ideas about group process that became widespread then. Some quite explicitly aim for the sorts of value Inglehart calls post-materialist. Therapeutic models have influenced most such groups, no matter what their specific fields of concern are. Self-help groups are particularly prominent. As with all groups and communities, small groups obviously have their limitations and problems, but they do give evidence of a rich civic life.

In his study of the UK in the post-1950 period, Peter Hall shows that activity in the third sector – voluntary work – has expanded over the past forty years. More traditional groups have declined, but they have been more than made up for by new ones, particularly self-help and environmental groups. A major change is the increased participation of women. Charitable groups have shown a considerable increase – there were over 160,000 registered charitable groups in Britain in 1991. Nearly 20 per cent of the population engages in some form of voluntary work during the course of the average year, and about 10 per cent do so on a weekly basis. Hall found that younger people are involved in voluntary work now at least as frequently as was the case in earlier generations.

Significantly, however, most of the increase in civic activity has happened among the more affluent strata. People from poorer backgrounds are more likely to centre their informal social contacts upon close kin. Much smaller proportions of people in the more affluent groups suffer from a complete absence of social support than do those in the poorer strata.[6]

One of the prime concerns of government involvement should be to help repair the civil order among such groups. The integrated working-class community is a persistent image, but now largely belongs to the past. Civic involvement is least developed in areas and neighbourhoods marginalized by the sweep of economic and social change. The renewal of deprived local communities presumes the encouragement of economic enterprise as a means of generating a broader civic recovery. The lessons of 1960s social engineering have by now been learned everywhere. Recent studies indicate that with appropriate external support, local initiative can reverse even strongly embedded processes of decline.[7]

Such studies come from many parts of the world, not just from Europe or the US. Ceara, in northeastern Brazil, is an instance.[8] The reforms in the area were initiated by a group of young business leaders, working in sectors such as television, retail marketing and services. The traditional elites in Ceara exported agricultural products abroad, and were interested more in keeping the wages down than in local development.

The reformers subsequently joined with government agencies, using participatory planning techniques and meeting community organizations. In order to promote indigenous development, schemes were set up to introduce new enterprises into the area. Families with the greatest need were allocated one minimum-wage job per household. Day-care centres were set up, run not by the government but by volunteers guaranteed at least the minimum wage. Neighbourhood groups and community organizations were given resources to lend on a small scale – for example, lending a woman money to buy a sewing machine so she can earn a living on her own. Between 1987 and 1994 Ceara's economy grew at a rate of 4 per cent, compared with 1.4 per cent for Brazil as a whole.

Social entrepreneurship is another case in point. An extraordinary variety of schemes of social entrepreneurship have grown up in different countries since the late 1980s. One is 'service credit', introduced in a range of cities in the US and Japan. Volunteers who take part in charitable work are 'paid' in time donated by other volunteer workers. A computer system registers every 'time dollar' earned and spent and provides participants with regular accounts. Time dollars are tax free and can be accumulated to pay for health care as well as other health services, including reducing health insurance costs. The Time Dollar Institute of New York is developing an employment agency that will provide access to job opportunities, training and support schemes. Individuals can use the agency to get job information, and receive a time dollar for every hour worked in addition to whatever orthodox wages the job pays. These can be banked and used either for educational courses or as a resource if the person becomes unemployed. A project initiated in 1998 will set up centres in fifty-two cities across the world to provide employer-supported volunteer programmes concerned with education and health. Based on time dollar programmes, it seeks to establish a volunteered time economy, using sophisticated computer technology.

Government should be prepared to contribute to such endeavours, as well as encourage other forms of bottom-up decision-making and local autonomy. Microcredit schemes, for example, have a proven effectiveness as a means of encouraging local economic initiatives. Some activities can be developed by local communities, but often need to be licensed or monitored by government. This is obviously true of education, for example, where schools might be given a range of new powers, but the way these are used has to be regulated by the state.

Sustained investment in inner city areas can create relevant work skills, develop local business ownership and provide capital for the refurbishment of building stock. Government can provide capital in a direct way, but also create incentives for private corporations to make investments, offer training programmes and foster local initiative. California among other states in the US has successful enterprise zones in operation, with others planned. Various further proposals have been suggested. One is to waive capital gains tax if profits are reinvested in businesses in such a way that shares are acquired by employees resident in enterprise zones. Another is to do so if the proceeds are reinvested in non-profit organizations that provide skills training or other community resources.

Policies of community renewal must not ignore the public sphere. An open public sphere is as important at local as at national level, and is one way in which democratization connects directly with community development. Without it, schemes of community renewal risk separating the community from the wider society, and are vulnerable to corruption. 'Public' here includes physical public space. The degeneration of local communities is usually marked not only by general dilapidation, but by the disappearance of safe public space – streets, squares, parks and other areas where people can feel secure.

The state can swamp civil society. This happened in the Communist economies of Eastern Europe and the Soviet Union, where there was no developed public sphere and where everyday sociability was largely confined to the home – usually there were few restaurants, cafés or public settings for social interaction. A healthy civil society protects the individual from overwhelming state power. Yet civil society is not, as some fondly imagine, a source of spontaneous order and harmony. Community regeneration can create its own problems and tensions. How much power should neighbourhood watch organizations have? What happens when local activist groups have very different versions of the community's future? Who decides where 'the community' ends and others begin? Government must adjudicate on these and other difficult questions. The state should also protect individuals from the conflicts of interest always present in civil society. The state couldn't devolve into civil society: 'if the state is everywhere, it is nowhere'.[9]

Crime and community

Preventing crime, and reducing fear of crime, are both closely related to community regeneration. One of the most significant innovations in criminology in recent years has been the discovery that the decay of day-to-day civility relates directly to criminality. For a long while attention was focused almost exclusively upon serious crime – robbery, assault or violence. More minor crimes and forms of public disorder, however, tend to have a cumulative effect. In European and American cities, when asked to describe their problems, residents of troubled neighbourhoods mention abandoned cars, graffiti, prostitution, youth gangs and similar phenomena.

People act on their anxieties about these issues: they leave the areas in question if they can, or they buy heavy locks for their doors and bars for their windows, and abandon public facilities. Disorderly behaviour unchecked signals to citizens that the area is unsafe. Fearful citizens stay off the streets, avoid certain neighbourhoods, and curtail their normal activities and associations. As they withdraw physically, they also withdraw from roles of mutual support with fellow citizens, thereby relinquishing the social controls that formerly helped to maintain civility within the community. 'Ultimately the result for a neighbourhood whose fabric of urban life and social intercourse has been undermined is increasing vulnerability to an influx of more disorderly behaviour and serious crime.'[10]

The implications of this thesis should be clearly understood. It does not mean increasing the powers of the police to sweep undesirables off the streets. Almost to the contrary, it means that the police should work closely with citizens to improve local community standards and civil behaviour, using education, persuasion and counselling instead of arraignment. In his recent book, lawyer Stephen Carter has charted the fate of civility in modern societies. Civility he defines as 'the sum of the many sacrifices we are called to make for the sake of living together'. It is about our relationships with strangers – feeling secure in encounters in public places with individuals we may never see more than once.[11]

It is frequently said that people tend to have an irrational fear of crime. Older people, especially those living in poorer areas, are often anxious about being mugged, when the chances of this happening are low. Young men are much more likely to be victims of assault than the elderly. However, this ignores the fact that people who fear crime alter their behaviour so as to avoid potentially threatening situations – not going out after dark and so on. The risk of being a victim of crime thus seems lower than it actually is.

Collaborative policing implies not only drawing in citizens themselves, but changing the characteristic outlook of police forces. Most countries have adopted the 'professional model of policing', introduced from the late 1950s onwards. 'Professional policing' involves concentrating mainly on serious crime and tackling it through the centralization of police authority, including on a transnational level. Yet the devolutionary implications of globalization apply in policing as in other spheres. A renewed emphasis upon crime prevention rather than law enforcement can go hand in hand with the reintegration of policing with the community. The isolation of the police from those they are supposed to serve often produces a siege mentality, since the police have little regular contact with ordinary citizens.

In order to work, partnerships between government agencies, the criminal justice system, local associations and community organizations have to be inclusive – all economic and ethnic groups must be involved.[12] Government and business can act together to help repair urban decay. One model is the creation of business improvement districts providing tax breaks for corporations that participate in strategic planning and offer investment in designated areas. To be successful, such schemes demand a long-term commitment to social objectives.

Emphasizing these strategies does not mean denying the links between unemployment, poverty and crime. Rather, the struggle against these social ills should be coordinated with community-based approaches to crime prevention. These approaches can in fact contribute directly and indirectly to furthering social justice. Where civil order has decayed along with public services and building stock, other opportunities

decline also. Improving the quality of life in a neighbourhood can revive them.

The democratic family

The family is a basic institution of civil society. Family
policy is a key test for the new politics: is there a politics of the family beyond neoliberalism and old-style
social democracy?

As with so many other areas, the backdrop is
change. The statistics are well known. Divorce has
risen steeply in almost all Western countries, although
rates in some are much higher than in others. The proportion of single-parent families and of children born
to non-married parents has gone up steadily. In the UK
in 1994, 32 per cent of births occurred outside marriage. While in Italy the rate was only 7 per cent, in
France it was 35 per cent, in Denmark 47 per cent and
in Sweden 50 per cent. The numbers of people living
alone have also risen. In many countries only a minority of children are now brought up in a 'traditional'
context, where father and mother are married and
living in the same household as their biological children, where the father is the economic breadwinner
and the mother a housewife.

Many now speak of the breakdown of the family. If
such a breakdown is occurring, it is extremely significant. The family is the meeting point of a range of
trends affecting society as a whole – increasing equality
between the sexes, the widespread entry of women into

the labour force, changes in sexual behaviour and expectations, the changing relationship between home and work.

The right has a particular story to tell about the consequences of these changes. The family is in crisis because the traditional family is disintegrating. The remedies proposed flow from this analysis. The sanctity of marriage should be reaffirmed. Marriage is the main emotional training ground for errant males, binding them into duties and responsibilities they would otherwise abandon. Fatherlessness, according to such a view, 'is the most harmful demographic trend of this generation ... It is also the engine driving our most urgent social problems from crime to adolescent pregnancy to child sexual abuse to domestic violence against women.'[13] To preserve the family, divorce should be made harder to obtain. Unorthodox family relationships, such as gay ones, should not receive support from either government or religious authorities, or should actively be discouraged. Homosexual marriage must continue to be legally outlawed. Welfare measures that encourage single-parent households should be reformed to remove this effect.

Many on the social democratic left, and also some libertarians, hold a very different view. For them the story of the contemporary family is one of healthy proliferation. After all, if diversity and choice are the watchwords of the age, why should these stop at the threshold of the family? We should accept that people can live happily together without being married, homosexuals can raise children just as competently as the heterosexual population, and, given adequate resources, single parents are able to bring up children just as satisfactorily as couples can.

How might the new politics approach the question of family? We should be clear first of all how implausible the idea of returning to the traditional family is. It is worth listing the reasons:

- We are dealing with profound processes of change in everyday life, which it is well beyond the capacity of any political agency to reverse.
- Nostalgia for the traditional family idealizes the past. Broken families were almost as common in the UK in the nineteenth century as now, although the main reason was death of a spouse rather than separation or divorce. Historical research is revealing more and more about the dark side of the traditional family, where violence against and sexual abuse of children were much more frequent than most historians used to believe.
- The traditional family was above all an economic and kinship unit. Marriage ties were not individualized as they are now, and love or emotional involvement was not the prime basis of marriage, as they have subsequently become.
- Traditional marriage was based upon the inequality of the sexes and the legal ownership of wives by husbands – women were chattels in English law until well into this century. Children similarly had few legal rights.
- The traditional family generally involved a sexual double standard. Married women were expected to be 'virtuous', partly because of the importance of

ensuring paternity. Men were allowed greater sexual licence.

- Children were the *raison d'être* of marriage. Large families were either desired or accepted as normal. We now live in the era of the 'prized child', where children are no longer an economic benefit but instead a major economic cost. The nature of childhood and child rearing has changed profoundly.

Recapturing the traditional family is a non-starter. Almost any of these points taken on its own would be enough to undermine such a project. It isn't surprising, therefore, that when rightist critics speak of the traditional family, they don't in fact mean the traditional family at all, but a transitional state of the family in the immediate post-war period – the (idealized) family of the 1950s. The traditional family by this point had all but disappeared, but women hadn't yet entered the labour force in large numbers and sexual inequalities remained pronounced.

Is the alternative view to the rightist one persuasive? No, because the notion that a proliferation of family forms is both desirable and unproblematic simply is not convincing. The effects of divorce on the lives of children will always be difficult to assess, because we don't know what would have happened had the parents stayed together. The most exhaustive set of studies carried out to date, however, rejects 'the claim that children raised by only one parent do just as well as children raised by both parents'.[14] A large part of the reason is economic – the sudden drop in income associated with divorce. But about half of the disadvantage comes from inadequate parental attention and lack of social ties. Separation or divorce, the authors show, weaken the connection between child and father, as well as the link between the child and the father's network of friends and acquaintances. On the basis of wide empirical research, the authors conclude it is a myth that there are usually strong support networks or extended family ties available to single mothers.

All is not well with marriage, the family and the care of children, but the question is what effective political strategies could improve them and what ideal state of the family we should strive for. First and most fundamentally we must start from the principle of equality between the sexes, from which there can be no going back. There is only one story to tell about the family today, and that is of democracy. The family is becoming democratized, in ways which track processes of public democracy; and such democratization suggests how family life might combine individual choice and social solidarity.

The criteria are surprisingly close. Democracy in the public sphere involves formal equality, individual rights, public discussion of issues free from violence, and authority which is negotiated rather than given by tradition. The democratized family shares these characteristics, some of which are already protected in national and international law. Democratization in the context of the family implies equality, mutual respect, autonomy, decision-making through communication and freedom from violence. Much the same characteristics also supply a model for parent–child relationships. Parents of course will still claim authority over children, and rightly so; but this will be more negotiated and open than before. These qualities do not apply only to heterosexual families – they have exactly the same purchase in homosexual relationships.

The democratized family is again an ideal. How should social democrats seek to promote that ideal and what specifically can government do? As elsewhere, the emphasis must surely be upon securing a balance of autonomy and responsibility in which positive forms of encouragement go along with other sanctions. There is a widespread yearning for the family to provide stability in a changing world, but realistically it is as likely to reflect other qualities of this world as compensate for them. Much stress is laid upon flexibility and adaptability in the workplace: the same needs to be true of capabilities individuals bring to marriage and family relationships. The capability to sustain relationships through change, even radical changes such as divorce, becomes central not only to individuals' happiness, but to the achievement of continuity in relationships with children.

The protection and care of children is the single most important thread that should guide family policy. It is not a solution to propose that divorce should be made more difficult to obtain. Such a measure might lower formal divorce rates but would not prevent separation and would almost certainly mean that even fewer people would marry – the opposite effect to that desired by those who advocate stricter divorce laws.

Democratic family relationships imply shared responsibility for child care, especially greater sharing among women and men, and among parents and nonparents, since in the society at large mothers are bearing a disproportionate share of the costs (and enjoying a disproportionate share of the emotional rewards) of children. Marriage and parenthood have always been thought of as tied together, but in the detraditionalized family, where having a child is an altogether different decision from in the past, the two are becoming disentangled. The proportion of children born outside marriage probably won't decline, and life-long sexual partnerships will almost certainly become increasingly uncommon. Contractual commitment to a child could thus be separated from marriage, and made by each parent as a binding matter of law, with unmarried and married fathers having the same rights and the same obligations.[15] Both sexes would have to recognize that sexual encounters carry the chance of life-time responsibilities, including protection from physical abuse. In combination with other cultural changes promoting a more positive image of fatherhood, such a restructuring of parenthood would undermine the very

---

The democratic family

Emotional and sexual equality
Mutual rights and responsibilities in relationships
Co-parenting
Life-long parental contracts
Negotiated authority over children
Obligations of children to parents
The socially integrated family

---

idea of the 'single parent'. Enforcing parenthood contracts wouldn't be without its problems. Obviously
other modes of seeking to balance risk and responsibility could also be instituted.

Democracy is difficult to achieve and can be hard to
live with, in the family as in other areas. As far as the
care of children is concerned, it implies co-parenting,
however far off this may be in current circumstances.
The rightist view of the disintegration of the traditional
family tends to go along with a specific thesis about the
limitations of men: men are intrinsically feckless and
morally irresponsible; unless safely locked into marriage of a traditional kind, they are a socially disruptive
force.

Yet research does not support this idea.[16] For most
men, as for women, divorce is a painful and distressing
experience. The large majority of men don't feel relief
at having shed their responsibilities for their children.
Most attempt to sustain their relationships with them,
even in the face of great difficulties. Many who lose
contact do so because of the emotional traumas
involved, or the active hostility of the ex-partner,
rather than a desire to follow an errant lifestyle.

As one researcher points out, there is a very thin line
between those fathers who remain closely involved
with their children after divorce and those who do not.
The most important determinant is not the attitude of
the father, but the responses of others, plus contingent
events which sway things one way rather than the
other. Many fathers do lose contact with their children
and do not support them economically. Contrary to the
'errant male' view, however, this does not seem to be a

gender issue. A study by the US Census Bureau found that non-custodial mothers were less likely than comparable fathers to pay child maintenance awarded by the courts.[17]

Co-parenting could be encouraged by a number of innovations. Like 'single mother', the term 'absent parent', widely used in law, helps perpetuate a situation where one parent, normally the father, is seen and treated as peripheral. Economic factors are also relevant. Why shouldn't child minding and out-of-school care be just as available for non-resident fathers as for single mothers? Fathers should have greater parenting rights than at present, but they should be provided, where necessary, with the means to discharge their responsibilities.

Politicians often speak of the need for strong families to promote social cohesion. They aren't wrong to do so, but some qualifications should be made. First, the family doesn't only refer to parents bringing up children. Children should have responsibilities to their parents, not just the other way round. It is worth at least considering whether this should be legally binding. The federal government in the US in 1983, in fact, sought to require children to help support ageing parents, as part of the Medicaid programme. The proposal was never implemented, although some twenty-six states now have statutes requiring children to provide support for needy parents.[18] While these have rarely been enforced, perhaps this is a notion whose time has come. For example, such obligations could be meshed with life-long parenting contracts.

Second, we don't need to look far to see that strong

families do not inevitably create social solidarity. Southern Italy provides an example on a large scale, but something similar can be true in other settings. Poor neighbourhoods, for instance, may have their own criminal families, where strong ties and obligations are the very basis of their law-breaking activities. Even perfectly law-abiding families may close themselves off from the wider world and abandon their responsibilities towards it. Strong family ties can be an effective source of civic cohesion only if they look outwards as well as inwards – this is what I mean by the socially integrated family. Family relations are part of the wider fabric of social life.

4

The Social Investment State

Classical social democracy thought of wealth creation as almost incidental to its basic concerns with economic security and redistribution. The neoliberals placed competitiveness and the generating of wealth much more to the forefront. Third way politics also gives very strong emphasis to these qualities, which have an urgent importance given the nature of the global marketplace. They will not be developed, however, if individuals are abandoned to sink or swim in an economic whirlpool. Government has an essential role to play in investing in the human resources and infrastructure needed to develop an entrepreneurial culture.

Third way politics, it could be suggested, advocates a *new mixed economy*. Two different versions of the old mixed economy existed. One involved a separation between state and private sectors, but with a good deal of industry in public hands. The other was and is the social market. In each of these, markets are kept largely subordinate to government. The new mixed economy looks instead for a synergy between public and private sectors, utilizing the dynamism of markets but with the public interest in mind. It involves a balance between regulation and deregulation, on a transnational as well as national and local levels; and a balance between the economic and the non-economic in the life of the society. The second of these is at least as important as the first, but attained in some part through it.

A high rate of business formation and dissolution is characteristic of a dynamic economy. This flux is not compatible with a society where taken-for-granted habits dominate, including those generated by welfare systems. Social democrats have to shift the relationship between *risk* and *security* involved in the welfare state, to develop a society of 'responsible risk takers' in the spheres of government, business enterprise and labour markets. People need protection when things go wrong, but also the material and moral capabilities to move through major periods of transition in their lives.

The issue of equality needs to be thought through carefully. Equality and individual liberty can come into conflict, and it is no good pretending that equality, pluralism and economic dynamism are always compatible. Driven as it is by structural changes, expanding inequality is not easy to combat. Social democrats should not accept, however, that high levels of inequality are functional for economic prosperity, or that they are inevitable. They should move away from what has sometimes been in the past an obsession with inequality, as well as rethink what equality is. Equality must contribute to diversity, not stand in its way.

For reasons I shall give below, redistribution must

not disappear from the agenda of social democracy. But recent discussion among social democrats has quite rightly shifted the emphasis towards the 'redistribution of possibilities'. The cultivation of human potential should as far as possible replace 'after the event' redistribution.

The meaning of equality

Many suggest that the only model of equality today should be equality of opportunity, or meritocracy – that is, the neoliberal model. It is important to be clear why this position is not tenable. In the first place (were it achievable), a radically meritocratic society would create deep inequalities of outcome, which would threaten social cohesion. Consider, for example, the winner-take-all phenomenon, a demonstrable effect in labour markets. Someone who is only marginally more talented than another person may command a larger salary than the other. A top tennis player or opera singer earns vastly more than one who isn't quite so good, and this happens, not in spite of, but because of the fact that a meritocratic principle is in operation. When barely perceptible margins make the difference between product success or failure, to a business the stakes are enormous. Individuals perceived to make this marginal difference are rewarded disproportionately. They are a new category of 'unknown celebrities.'[1]

Unless it goes along with a structural change in the distribution of jobs, which by definition can only be transitory, a meritocratic society would also have a great deal of downward mobility. Many must move down for others to move up. Yet as much research has shown, widespread downward mobility has socially dislocating consequences, and produces feelings of alienation among those affected. Large-scale downward mobility would be as threatening to social cohesion as would the existence of a disaffected class of the excluded. In fact, a full meritocracy would create an extreme example of such a class, a class of untouchables. For not only would groups of people be at the bottom, but they would know their lack of ability made this right and proper: it is hard to imagine anything more dispiriting.

In any case, a fully meritocratic society is not only unrealizable; it is a self-contradictory idea. For reasons already given, a meritocratic society is likely to be highly unequal on the level of outcome. In such a social order, the privileged are bound to be able to confer advantages on their children – thus destroying meritocracy. After all, even in the relatively egalitarian Soviet-style societies, where wealth couldn't secure the advancement of children, privileged groups were able to transmit advantages to their offspring.

These observations don't imply that meritocratic principles are irrelevant to equality, but they do mean that these principles can't be exhaustive of it, or be used to define it. What then should equality be taken to mean? The new politics defines equality as *inclusion* and inequality as *exclusion*, although these terms need some spelling out. Inclusion refers in its broadest sense to citizenship, to the civil and political rights and obligations that all members of a society should have, not just formally, but as a reality of their lives. It also refers to opportunities and to involvement in public space. In a society where work remains central to self-esteem and standard of living, access to work is one main context of opportunity. Education is another, and would be so even if it weren't so important for the employment possibilities to which it is relevant.

Two forms of exclusion are becoming marked in contemporary societies. One is the exclusion of those at the bottom, cut off from the mainstream of opportunities society has to offer. At the top is voluntary exclusion, the 'revolt of the elites': a withdrawal from public institutions on the part of more affluent groups, who choose to live separately from the rest of the society.[2] Privileged groups start to live in fortress communities, and pull out from public education and public health systems.

Inclusion and exclusion have become important concepts for analysing and responding to inequality because of changes affecting the class structure of the industrial countries, referred to briefly earlier. A quarter of a century ago a majority of the working population were in manual jobs, mostly in manufacture. Information technology has drastically affected the nature of manufacturing production, and cut the demand for unskilled labour dramatically. Computer-aided design and customization, automated storage and distribution systems, and the integration of production with suppliers and customers have all replaced work previously done by hand. Today less than 20 per cent of the workforce in most of the developed economies is in manufacture, and the proportion is continuing to fall. The traditional working class has largely disappeared and the old working-class communities, centred for example on coal, iron and steel production or shipbuilding, have altered their character.

Some have been revitalized, while others have sunk into decline. Like depressed inner city neighbourhoods, these have become isolated from the wider society. Where there is a strong presence of minority groups, ethnic prejudice can further reinforce exclusionary processes. As American cities long have done, cities in Europe are drawing in large numbers of immigrants, creating a 'new poor' in London, Paris, Berlin, Rome and other urban areas. Economic exclusion is thus often also physical and cultural. In declining areas, housing falls into disrepair, and lack of job opportunities produces education disincentives, leading to social instability and disorganization. More than 60 per cent of tenants on a string of council estates around the City of London, the richest square mile in Britain, are unemployed. Yet City Airport, very close by, cannot find enough skilled workers for its needs.[3]

Inclusion and exclusion

Exclusion is not about gradations of inequality, but about mechanisms that act to detach groups of people from the social mainstream. At the top, voluntary exclusion is driven by a diversity of factors. Having the economic means to pull out of the wider society is the necessary condition for, but never the whole explanation

---

The inclusive society

Equality as inclusion
Limited meritocracy
Renewal of public space (civic liberalism)
'Beyond the work society'
Positive welfare
The social investment state

---

as to why, groups choose to do so. Exclusion at the top is not only just as threatening for public space, or common solidarity, as exclusion at the bottom; it is causally linked to it. That the two go together is easily seen from the more extreme examples that have developed in some countries, such as Brazil or South Africa. Limiting the voluntary exclusion of the elites is central to creating a more inclusive society at the bottom.

Many suggest the accumulation of privilege at the top is unstoppable. Income inequalities seem to be rising across a wide front. In the US, for example, 60 per cent of income gains over the period from 1980 to 1990 went to the top 1 per cent of the population, while the real income of the poorest 25 per cent has remained static more or less for thirty years. The UK shows similar trends in less extreme form. The gap between the highest-paid and lowest-paid workers is greater than it has been for at least fifty years. While the large majority of the working population are better off in real terms than twenty years ago, the poorest 10 per cent have seen their real incomes decline.

Yet it does not follow that such trends are set to continue or worsen. Technological innovation is imponderable, and it is possible that at some point the tendency towards greater inequality might shift the other way. These trends are in any case more complicated than appears at first sight. As measured by some of the most exhaustive studies, income inequality has gone down rather than up in some developed countries over the past thirty years. Of course, we don't know exactly how reliable income data are – attempts to measure the secondary economy are guesswork. That economy may increase inequality, but it is more likely to act the other way, because informal economic activities, barter and unofficial cash transactions are normally more common among poorer groups. Finally, those countries having lengthy periods of neoliberal government have shown higher increases in economic inequality than others, with the US, New Zealand and the UK leading the way.

Writing in relation to the US, the political journalist Mickey Kaus has suggested a distinction between 'economic liberalism' and 'civic liberalism'.[4] The gap between rich and poor will keep growing and no one can stop it. The public realm, however, can be rebuilt through 'civic liberalism'. Kaus is surely right to argue that the emptying of public space can be reversed, and that tackling social exclusion at the top isn't only an economic issue. Yet economic inequalities are certainly not irrelevant to exclusionary mechanisms and we don't have to give up on reducing them.

In the context of Europe, one key element is sustaining levels of welfare spending. The welfare state might stand in need of radical reform, but welfare systems do and should influence resource distribution. Other strategies can also be contemplated, some of them capable of wide application, such as employee stock ownership schemes, the redistributive implications of which might be substantial. A basic influence upon the distribution of income is growing sexual equality. Here income inequality is decreasing, not increasing, contradicting again the simple statement that society is becoming more unequal. Changes in the family affect structures of inequality. Thus in the UK in 1994–5, half of those in the top 20 per cent of incomes were either single full-time workers or couples both working full-time. The new patterns of inequality are not just given. They can be influenced by government policies, such as ones that support the involvement of single parents in the labour force.

'Civic liberalism' – the recapturing of public space – none the less must be a basic part of an inclusive society at the top. How can this liberalism be renewed or sustained? The successful cultivation of the cosmopolitan nation is one way. People who feel themselves members of a national community are likely to acknowledge a commitment to others within it. The development of a responsible business ethos is also relevant. In terms of social solidarity, the most important groups are not only the new corporate rich but also the members of the professional and moneyed middle class, since they are closest to the dividing lines which threaten to pull away from public space. Improving the quality of public education, sustaining a well-resourced health service, promoting safe public amenities, and controlling levels of crime are all relevant. It is for these reasons that reform of the welfare state should not reduce it to a safety net. Only a welfare system that benefits most of the population will generate a common morality of citizenship. Where 'welfare' assumes only a negative connotation, and is targeted largely at the poor, as has tended to happen in the US, the results are divisive.

The United States has a higher level of economic inequality than any other industrial country. Yet even in that society, the homeland of competitive individualism, there is cause for hope that the 'revolt of the elites' can be contained. In his recent research, the sociologist Alan Wolfe found little evidence that upper-middle-class people were seceding from the wider society. He discovered broad-based support in America for social justice, 'as likely to be shared by conservative Christians as by East Coast liberals'.[5] Most believe economic inequality in the US is getting too extreme:

> Economists who espouse a laissez faire approach to their discipline have been inclined to argue that high CEO salaries, even when seemingly outrageous, benefit everyone eventually, since inefficient companies or underpaid executives serve no-one's real interests. But from the perspective of middle class America, high corporate salaries are more likely to be viewed as selfish, and selfish people and organisations, because they are out of balance, threaten the delicacy of the social order.[6]

It isn't difficult to think of policies that will have a positive effect on public space rather than corroding it.

Health care, for example, should correspond to the needs of a wide constituency. 'Health care' here should be taken in a wide sense, commensurate with the idea of positive welfare to be discussed later. The reduction of environmental pollution, for example, is a general benefit. Indeed ecological strategies are a core element of lifestyle bargains, since most ecological benefits cut across classes.

Like social exclusion at the top, exclusion at the bottom tends to be self-reproducing. Any strategies which break poverty cycles should be pursued:

> It is ... absolutely essential to help adults without basic skills or qualifications to acquire them, to help people whose skills are out of date to update them, and to raise the confidence of anyone whose morale has been undermined by a long period away from employment. People without skills are five times more likely to become unemployed than those with higher educational level qualifications; in the end employment goes to the employable.[7]

Education and training have become the new mantra for social democratic politicians. Tony Blair famously describes his three main priorities in government as 'education, education, education'. The need for improved education skills and skills training is apparent in most industrial countries, particularly as far as poorer groups are concerned. Who could gainsay that a well-educated population is desirable for any society? Investment in education is an imperative of government today, a key basis of the 'redistribution of possibilities'. Yet the idea that education can reduce inequalities in a direct way should be regarded with some scepticism. A great deal of comparative research, in the US and Europe, demonstrates that education tends to reflect wider economic inequalities and these have to be tackled at source.

Involvement in the labour force, and not just in dead-end jobs, is plainly vital to attacking involuntary exclusion. Work has multiple benefits: it generates income for the individual, gives a sense of stability and direction in life, and creates wealth for the overall society. Yet inclusion must stretch well beyond work, not only because there are many people at any one time not able to be in the labour force, but because a society too dominated by the work ethic would be a thoroughly unattractive place in which to live. An inclusive society must provide for the basic needs of those who can't work, and must recognize the wider diversity of goals life has to offer.

Conventional poverty programmes need to be replaced with community-focused approaches, which permit more democratic participation as well as being more effective. Community building emphases support networks, self-help and the cultivation of social capital as means to generate economic renewal in low-income neighbourhoods. Fighting poverty requires an injection of economic resources, but applied to support local initiative. Leaving people mired in benefits tends to exclude them from the larger society. Reducing benefits to force individuals into work pushes them into already crowded low-wage labour markets. Community building initiatives concentrate upon the multiple problems individuals and families face, including job quality, health and child care, education and transport.[8]

A society of positive welfare

No issue has polarized left and right more profoundly in recent years than the welfare state, extolled on the one side and excoriated on the other. What became 'the welfare state' (a term not in widespread use until the 1960s and one William Beveridge, the architect of the British welfare state, thoroughly disliked) has in fact a chequered history. Its origins were far removed from the ideals of the left – indeed it was created partly to dispel the socialist menace. The ruling groups who set up the social insurance system in imperial Germany in the late nineteenth century despised laissez-faire economics as much as they did socialism. Yet Bismarck's model was copied by many countries. Beveridge visited Germany in 1907 in order to study the model.[9] The welfare state as it exists today in Europe was produced in and by war, as were so many aspects of national citizenship.

The system Bismarck created in Germany is usually taken as the classic form of the welfare state. Yet the welfare state in Germany has always had a complex network of third sector groups and associations that the authorities have depended on for putting welfare policies into practice. The aim is to help these to attain their social objectives. In areas such as child care, third sector groups have almost a monopoly on provision. The non-profit sector in Germany expanded rather than shrank as the welfare state grew. Welfare states vary in the degree to which they incorporate or rely upon the third sector. In Holland, for instance, non-profit organizations are the main delivery system for social services, while in Sweden hardly any are used. In Belgium and Austria, as in Germany, about half the social services are provided by non-profit groups.

The Dutch political scientist Kees van Kersbergen argues that 'one of the major insights of the contemporary debate [about the welfare state] is that to equate social democracy and the welfare state may have been a mistake'.[10] He examines in detail the influence of Christian democracy upon the development of Continental welfare systems and the social market. The Christian democratic parties descend from the Catholic parties that were important between the wars in Germany, Holland, Austria and to a lesser degree France and Italy. The Catholic unionists saw socialism as the enemy and sought to outflank it on its own ground by stressing codetermination and class reconciliation. Ronald Reagan's view, expressed in 1981, that 'we have let government take away those things that were once ours to do voluntarily' finds a much earlier echo in Europe in the Catholic tradition. Church, family and friends are the main sources of social solidarity. The state should step in only when those institutions don't fully live up to their obligations.

Recognizing the problematic history of the welfare state, third way politics should accept some of the criticisms the right makes of that state. It is essentially undemocratic, depending as it does upon a top-down distribution of benefits. Its motive force is protection and care, but it does not give enough space to personal liberty. Some forms of welfare institution are bureaucratic, alienating and inefficient, and welfare benefits can create perverse consequences that undermine what they were designed to achieve. However, third way politics sees these problems not as a signal to dismantle the welfare state, but as part of the reason to reconstruct it.

The difficulties of the welfare state are only partly financial. In most Western societies, proportional expenditure on welfare systems has remained quite stable over the past ten years. In the UK, the share of GDP spent on the welfare state increased steadily for most of the century up to the late 1970s. Since then it has stabilized,[11] although the gross figures conceal changes in the distribution of spending and the sources of revenue. The resilience of welfare budgets in the UK is all the more remarkable given the determination of Margaret Thatcher's governments to cut them.

Expenditure on education as a percentage of GDP fell between 1975 and 1995 from 6.7 per cent to 5.2 per cent. Spending on the health service, however, rose over this period. In 1975 it was equivalent to 3.8 per cent of GDP. By 1995 it had risen to 5.7 per cent (a lower percentage than in most other industrial countries). Public housing experienced the greatest cut, declining from 4.2 per cent of GDP in 1975 to 2.1 per cent twenty years later. As happened elsewhere, spending on social security increased most. In 1973–4 it made up 8.2 per cent of GDP. This reached 11.4 per cent by 1995–6. Expenditure on social security went up by more than 100 per cent in real terms over the period. The main factors underlying the increase were high unemployment, a growth in the numbers of in-work poor, and changes in demographic patterns, especially a growth in numbers of single parents and older people.

Much the same developments have affected all welfare systems, since they are bound up with structural changes of a profound kind. They are causing basic problems for the more comprehensive welfare states, such as those in Scandinavia. Nordic egalitarianism has historical and cultural roots rather than being only the product of the universalist welfare state. There is a wider public acceptance of high levels of taxation than in most Western countries. But the benefits system comes under strain whenever unemployment rises, as happened in Finland – this in spite of the fact that the Nordic countries pioneered active labour market policies. Given its relative size, the Scandinavian welfare state is a major employer, particularly of women. Yet as a result the degree of sexual segregation in employment is higher than in most other industrial countries.

The large increase in social security spending is one of the main sources of attack on welfare systems by neoliberals, who see in it the widespread development of welfare dependency. They are surely correct to worry about the number of people who live off state benefits, but there is a more sophisticated way of looking at what is going on. Welfare prescriptions quite often become sub-optimal, or set up situations of moral hazard. The idea of moral hazard is widely used in discussions of risk in private insurance. Moral hazard exists when people use insurance protection to alter their behaviour, thereby redefining the risk for which they are insured. It isn't so much that some forms of welfare provision create dependency cultures as that people take rational advantage of opportunities offered. Benefits meant to counter unemployment, for instance, can actually produce unemployment if they are actively used as a shelter from the labour market.

Writing against the backdrop of the Swedish welfare system, the economist Assar Lindbeck notes that a strong humanitarian case can be made for generous support for people affected by unemployment, illness, disability or the other standard risks covered by the welfare state. The dilemma is that the higher the benefits the greater will be the chance of moral hazard, as well as fraud. He suggests that moral hazard tends to be greater in the long run than in shorter time periods. This is because in the longer term social habits are built up which come to define what is 'normal'. Serious benefit dependency is then no longer even seen as such but simply becomes 'expected' behaviour. An increased tendency to apply for social assistance, more absence from work for alleged health reasons, and a lower level of job search may be among the results.[12]

Once established, benefits have their own autonomy, regardless of whether or not they meet the purposes for which they were originally designed. As this happens, expectations become 'locked in' and interest groups entrenched. Countries that have tried to reform their pensions systems, for example, have met with concerted resistance. We should have our pensions because we are 'old' (at age 60 or 65), we have paid our dues (even if they don't cover the costs), other people before have had them, everyone looks forward to retirement and so forth. Yet such institutional stasis is in and of itself a reflection of the need for reform, for the welfare state needs to be as dynamic and responsive to wider social trends as any other sector of government.

Welfare reform isn't easy to achieve, precisely because of the entrenched interests that welfare systems create. Yet the outline of a radical project for the welfare state can be sketched out quite readily.

The welfare state, as indicated earlier, is a pooling of risk rather than resources. What has shaped the solidarity of social policy is that 'otherwise privileged groups discovered that they shared a common interest in reallocating risk with the disadvantaged'.[13] However, the welfare state isn't geared up to cover new-style risks such as those concerning technological change, social exclusion or the accelerating proportion of one-parent households. These mismatches are of two kinds: where risks covered don't fit with needs, and where the wrong groups are protected.

Welfare reform should recognize the points about risk made earlier in the discussion: effective risk management (individual or collective) doesn't just mean minimizing or protecting against risks; it also means harnessing the positive or energetic side of risk and providing resources for risk taking. Active risk taking is recognized as inherent in entrepreneurial activity, but the same applies to the labour force. Deciding to go to work and give up benefits, or taking a job in a particular industry, are risk-infused activities – but such risk taking is often beneficial both to the individual and to the wider society.

The Social Investment State

When Beveridge wrote his *Report on Social Insurance and Allied Services*, in 1942, he famously declared war on Want, Disease, Ignorance, Squalor and Idleness. In other words, his focus was almost entirely negative. We should speak today of *positive welfare*, to which individuals themselves and other agencies besides government contribute – and which is functional for wealth creation. Welfare is not in essence an economic concept, but a psychic one, concerning as it does well-being. Economic benefits or advantages are therefore virtually never enough on their own to create it. Not only is welfare generated by many contexts and influences other than the welfare state, but welfare institutions must be concerned with fostering psychological as well as economic benefits. Quite mundane examples can be given: counselling, for example, might sometimes be more helpful than direct economic support.

Although these propositions may sound remote from the down-to-earth concerns of welfare systems, there isn't a single area of welfare reform to which they aren't relevant or which they don't help illuminate. The guideline is investment in *human capital* wherever possible, rather than the direct provision of economic maintenance. In place of the welfare state we should put the *social investment state*, operating in the context of a positive welfare society.

The theme that the 'welfare state' should be replaced by the 'welfare society' has become a conventional one in the recent literature on welfare issues. Where third sector agencies are not already well represented, they should play a greater part in providing welfare services.

117

The top-down dispensation of benefits should cede place to more localized distribution systems. More generally, we should recognize that the reconstruction of welfare provision has to be integrated with programmes for the active development of civil society.

Social investment strategies

Since the institutions and services ordinarily grouped together under the rubric of the welfare state are so many, I shall limit myself here to comments on social security. What would the social investment state aim for in terms of its social security systems? Let us take two basic areas: provision for old age and unemployment.

As regards old age, a radical perspective would suggest breaking out of the confines within which debate about pension payments is ordinarily carried on. Most industrial societies have ageing populations, and this is a big problem, it is said, because of the pensions time bomb. The pension commitments of some countries, such as Italy, Germany or Japan, are way beyond what can be afforded, even allowing for reasonable economic growth. If other societies, such as Britain, have to some extent avoided this difficulty, it is because they have actively reduced their state pension commitments – in Britain, for example, by indexing pensions to average prices rather than average earnings.

An adequate level of state-provided pension is a necessity. There is good reason also to support schemes of compulsory saving. In the UK the effect of relating pension increases to prices rather than earnings, without other statutory provisions, is likely to leave many retirees impoverished. A man who is 50 in 1998 and leaves the labour market aged 65 will receive a government pension amounting to only 10 per cent of average male earnings. Many people don't have either occupational or private pensions.[14] Other countries have come up with more effective strategies. A number of examples of combined public/private sector funding of pensions exist, some of which are capable of generalization. The Finnish system, for example, combines a state-guaranteed basic minimum income and earnings-related pension with regulated private sector provision.

The interest of the pensions issue, however, stretches more broadly than the questions of who should pay, at what level and by what means. It should go along with rethinking what old age is and how changes in the wider society affect the position of older people. Positive welfare applies as much in this context as in any other: it isn't enough to think only in terms of economic benefits. Old age is a new-style risk masquerading as an old-style one. Ageing used to be more passive than it is now: the ageing body was simply something that had to be accepted. In the more active, reflexive society, ageing has become much more of an open process, on a physical as well as a psychic level. Becoming older presents at least as many opportunities as problems, both for individuals and for the wider social community.

The concept of a pension that begins at retirement

age, and the label 'pensioner', were inventions of the welfare state. But not only do these not conform to the new realities of ageing, they are as clear a case of welfare dependency as one can find. They suggest incapacity, and it is not surprising that for many people retirement leads to a loss of self-esteem. When retirement first fixed 'old age' at 60 or 65, the situation of older people was very different from what it is now. In 1900, average life expectancy for a male aged 20 in England was only 62.

We should move towards abolishing the fixed age of retirement, and we should regard older people as a resource rather than a problem. The category of pensioner will then cease to exist, because it is detachable from pensions as such: it makes no sense to lock up pension funds against reaching 'pensionable age'. People should be able to use such funds as they wish – not only to leave the labour force at any age, but to finance education, or reduced working hours, when bringing up young children.[15] Abolishing statutory retirement would probably be neutral in respect of labour market implications, given that individuals could give up work earlier as well as stay in work longer. These provisions won't as such help pay for pensions where a country has overstretched its future commitments, and this perspective is agnostic about what balance should be aimed for between public and private funding. Yet it does suggest there is scope for innovative thinking around the pensions issue.

A society that separates older people from the majority in a retirement ghetto cannot be called inclusive. The precept of philosophic conservatism applies here as elsewhere: old age shouldn't be seen as a time of rights without responsibilities. Burke famously observed that 'society is a partnership not only between those who are living, but between those who are living, those who are dead and those who are to be born'.[16] Such a partnership is presumed, in a relatively mundane context, by the very idea of collective pensions, which act as a conduit between generations. But an intergenerational contract plainly needs to be deeper than this. The young should be willing to look to the old for models, and older people should see themselves as in the service of future generations.[17] Are such goals realistic in a society that has retreated from deference, and where age no longer appears to bring wisdom? Several factors suggest they may be. Being 'old' lasts longer than it used to do. There are far more old people in the population and hence the old are more socially visible. Finally, their growing involvement in work and the community should act to link them directly to younger generations.

The position of the frail elderly, people who need continuous care, raises more difficult questions. There are twenty times more people over 85 in the UK today than there were in 1900. Many of the 'young old' may be in quite a different situation from that of those in the same age group a couple of generations ago. It is a different matter for the 'old old', some of whom fare badly.[18] The question of what collective resources should be made available to the frail elderly is not just one of rationing. There are issues to be confronted here, including ethical questions of a quite fundamental sort, that go well beyond the scope of this discussion.

What of unemployment? Does the goal of full employment mean anything any more? Is there a straight trade-off, as the neoliberals say, between employment and deregulated labour markets – contrasting the US 'jobs miracle' with Eurosclerosis? We should note first of all that no simple comparison between the 'US' and the 'European model' is possible. As economist Stephen Nickell has shown, labour markets in Europe show great diversity. Over the period from 1983 to 1996, there were large variations in unemployment rates in OECD Europe, ranging from 1.8 per cent in Switzerland to over 20 per cent in Spain. Of OECD countries, 30 per cent over these years had average unemployment rates lower than the US. Those with the lowest rates are not noted for having the most deregulated labour markets (Austria, Portugal, Norway). Labour market rigidities like strict employment legislation don't strongly influence unemployment. High unemployment is linked to generous benefits that run on indefinitely and to poor educational standards at the lower end of the labour market – the phenomenon of exclusion.[19]

The position of the third way should be that sweeping deregulation is not the answer. Welfare expenditure should remain at European rather than US levels, but be switched as far as possible towards human capital investment. Benefit systems should be reformed where they induce moral hazard, and a more active risk-taking attitude encouraged, wherever possible through incentives, but where necessary by legal obligations.

It is worth perhaps at this stage commenting briefly on the 'Dutch model', sometimes pointed to as a successful adaptation of social democracy to new social and economic conditions. In an agreement concluded at Wassenaar some sixteen years ago, the country's unions agreed to wage moderation in exchange for a gradual reduction in working hours. As a result, labour costs have fallen by over 30 per cent over the last ten years, while the economy has thrived. This has been achieved with an unemployment rate below 6 per cent in 1997.

Looked at more closely, however, the Dutch model is less impressive, at least in terms of job creation and welfare reform. Substantial numbers who would in other countries count as unemployed are living on disability benefit – the country in fact has more people registered as unfit for work than it has officially unemployed. At 51 per cent, the proportion of the population aged 15–64 in full-time work is below what it was in 1970, when it was nearly 60 per cent and well short of the European average of 67 per cent. Of jobs created over the past ten years, 90 per cent are part-time. Holland spends the highest proportion of its income on social security of any European country, and its welfare system is under considerable strain.[20]

Strategies for job creation and the future of work need to be based upon an orientation to the new economic exigencies. Companies and consumers are increasingly operating on a world scale in terms of the standards demanded for goods and services. Consumers shop on a world level, in the sense that distribution is global and therefore 'the best' no longer has any generic connection with where goods and services are produced. Pressures to meet these standards will also apply more and more to labour forces. In some contexts such pressures are likely to deepen processes of social exclusion. The differentiation will be not only between manual and knowledge workers, or between high skills and low skills, but between those who are local in outlook and those who are more cosmopolitan.

Investment in human resources is proving to be the main source of leverage which firms have in key economic sectors. One study in the US compared 700 large companies across different industries. The results showed that even a marginal difference in an index of investment in people increased shareholder returns by $41,000.[21] The business analyst Rosabeth Moss Kanter identifies five main areas where government policy can assist job creation. There should be support for *entrepreneurial initiatives* concerned with small business startups and technological innovation. Many countries, particularly in Europe, still place too much reliance upon established economic institutions, including the public sector, to produce employment. In a world 'where customers can literally shop for workers', without the new ideas guaranteed by entrepreneurship there is an absence of competition. Entrepreneurship is a direct source of jobs. It also drives technological development, and gives people opportunities for self-employment in times of transition. Government policy can provide direct support for entrepreneurship, through helping create venture capital, but also through restructuring welfare systems to give security when entrepreneurial ventures go wrong – for example, by giving people the option to be taxed on a two- or three-year cycle rather than only annually.

The Social Investment State

Governments need to emphasize *life-long education*, developing education programmes that start from an individual's early years and continue on even late in life. Although training in specific skills may be necessary for many job transitions, more important is the development of cognitive and emotional competence. Instead of relying on unconditional benefits, policies should be oriented to encourage saving, the use of educational resources and other personal investment opportunities.

Public project partnerships can give private enterprise a larger role in activities which governments once provided for, while ensuring that the public interest remains paramount. The public sector can in turn provide resources that can help enterprise to flourish and without which joint projects may fail. Moss Kanter points out that welfare to work programmes in the US have sometimes foundered on the problem of transport. Companies offer jobs in areas which those available for them can't easily reach because of lack of adequate transport facilities.

Government policies can enhance *portability*, whether through common standards of education or through portable pension rights. Greater harmonization of educational practices and standards, for instance, is desirable for a cosmopolitan labour force. Some global corporations have already set up standardized entrance requirements, but governments need to take the lead. As in other areas, harmonization is not necessarily the enemy of educational diversity and may even be the condition of sustaining it.

Finally, governments should encourage *family-friendly workplace policies*, something that can also be achieved through public–private collaborations. Countries vary widely in the level of child care they offer, for instance, as do companies. Not only child care, but other work opportunities, such as telecommuting or work sabbaticals, can help reconcile employment and domestic life. The more companies emphasize human resources, the more competition there will be to have the best family-friendly work environments. Governments which help them will also tend to attract inward investment.[22]

Can these strategies produce a return to full employment in the usual sense – enough good jobs to go around for everyone who wants one? No one knows, but it seems unlikely. The proportion of jobs that are full-time and long-term is declining in Western economies. Comparisons between the 'full employment economies', such as the US or the UK, and 'high unemployment' societies, like Germany or France, are less clear cut when we compare not the number of jobs but the hours of work created. Net job creation for skilled work that is secure and well paid over the ten years 1986–96 was the same in Germany as in the US, at 2.6 per cent. Labour productivity doubled in Germany over that period, whereas in the US it rose by only 25 per cent.[23]

Since no one can say whether or not global capitalism will in future generate sufficient work, it would be foolish to proceed as though it will. Is the 'active redistribution' of work possible without counterproductive consequences? Probably not in the form of limits to the working week fixed by government – the difficulties with such schemes are well known. But if we see it in a wider context, we have no need to ask whether redistribution of work is possible. It is already happening on a widespread basis, and the point is to foster its positive aspects. One much-quoted experiment is that at Hewlett Packard's plant in Grenoble. The plant is kept open on a 24-hour cycle seven days a week. The employees have a working week averaging just over 30 hours, but receive the same wages as when they were working a 37.5-hour week. Labour productivity has increased substantially.[24]

Since the revival of civic culture is a basic ambition of third way politics, the active involvement of government in the social economy makes sense. Indeed some have presented the choice before us in stark terms, given the problematic status of full employment: either greater participation in the social economy or facing the growth of 'outlaw cultures'. The possibilities are many, including the time dollar schemes mentioned earlier and shadow wages – tax breaks for hours worked in the social economy. As diverse studies across Europe show, 'more and more people are looking both for meaningful work and opportunities for commitment outside of work. If society can upgrade and reward such commitment and put it on a level with gainful employment, it can create both individual identity and social cohesion.'[25]

In sum, what would a radically reformed welfare state – the social investment state in the positive welfare society – look like? Expenditure on welfare, understood as positive welfare, will be generated and distributed not wholly through the state, but by the state working in combination with other agencies, including business. The welfare society here is not just the nation, but stretches above and below it. Control of environmental pollution, for example, can never be a matter for national government alone, but it is certainly directly relevant to welfare. In the positive welfare society, the contract between individual and government shifts, since autonomy and the development of self – the medium of expanding individual responsibility – become the prime focus. Welfare in this basic sense concerns the rich as well as the poor.

Positive welfare would replace each of Beveridge's negatives with a positive: in place of Want, autonomy; not Disease but active health; instead of Ignorance, education, as a continuing part of life; rather than Squalor, well-being; and in place of Idleness, initiative.

5

Into the Global Age

Social democrats should seek a new role for the nation in a cosmopolitan world. The emerging global order cannot sustain itself as a 'pure marketplace'. The marketplace fragments as much as it unifies: a world of a thousand city-states, which some have predicted, would be unstable and dangerous. A reassertion of the role of the nation is important as a stabilizing force, a counter to endless fragmentation. Identity and belonging plainly are potentially divisive. How realistic is it to suppose that affiliation to the nation can be a benign force? After all, the nation-state and nationalism famously have a Janus face – nations provide an integrative mechanism of citizenship, but nationalism can become belligerent and nationalist aspirations have fed many destructive conflicts over the past century and a half.

The divisive aspects of nationalism won't disappear, of course. But it is exactly a more cosmopolitan version of nationhood we need to keep them in check. Such a cosmopolitanism is both cause and condition of the possible disappearance of large-scale war between nation-states. The 'strong state' used to be one well prepared for war. It must mean something different today: a nation sure enough of itself to accept the new limits of sovereignty.

The cosmopolitan nation

Nation-states were first formed when they developed clear 'borders', rather than the vaguer 'frontiers' characteristic of more traditional states. Borders are precise lines drawn on a map, which designate the territory of the nation, and any violation of them is regarded as an assault upon the nation's integrity. States are again coming to have frontiers rather than borders, but not for the same reasons as in the past. Early states had frontiers because they had an inadequate political apparatus: they couldn't make their authority count at their outer perimeters. The borders of current states are becoming frontiers because of their ties to other regions and their involvement with transnational groupings of all kinds. The European Union is the prototype, but the softening of boundaries is happening in other parts of the world too.

National identity can be a benign influence only if it is tolerant of ambivalence, or multiple affiliation. Individuals who simultaneously are English, British, European, and have some overall sense of global citizenship, may regard one of these as their overriding identity, but this need not prevent them accepting the others too. Xenophobic nationalism is the opposite: the nation is 'one, indivisible'. It is culturally protectionist, assuming the nation has a 'destiny' – that it is not only set apart from but superior to other nations. But nations don't have destinies and all nations, without exception, are 'mongrel nations'. The nation is not something given in nature, and whatever remote connections they may have to earlier ethnic communities, nations are a product of relatively recent history. They have all been built from a diversity of cultural fragments.

In his work on nationalism the political philosopher David Miller sets out to counter two widely held views on the left about the nation and nationalism. One is that nationalism is essentially a matter of feeling or emotion and devoid of rational content. The second is that nationalism is intrinsically a doctrine of the political right, hostile to left values. Those who hold such views, he argues, tend to treat nationalism as all of a piece, whereas in fact we can fairly readily distinguish different forms. 'The principle of nationality' rests upon a number of claims. National identities are a valid source of personal identity; individuals who experience being part of a nation as an element of their identity are not suffering from an illusion. It is morally defensible for them to wish to protect their identity against forces that might threaten it. Nations are ethical communities, where those involved owe special obligations to other members not always owed to others on the outside. Nations provide a focus for self-determination: the nation should develop state structures that allow citizens to decide for themselves matters of general importance.

131

Nations bring together these three elements with particular cogency because of certain other special qualities:

> nations are not voluntary associations, but communities within which most members are born, live and die, so that we are bound together with our compatriots in a community of fate; moreover, these communities . . . conceive of themselves as historically extended, so our obligations are not only to contemporaries but to past and future members as well . . . we must hold on to the principle of nationality, while striving to forge national identities that can accommodate the pluralism and mutability of contemporary culture.[1]

But how can this happen? Can the idea of the nation be compatible with ethnic and cultural pluralism? In response to this question, conservative nationalism holds that the 'unitary nation' must reign supreme – the 'one nation' is inherited from the past and must be protected from cultural contamination. The price of national community, as one rightist author puts it, is 'sanctity, intolerance, exclusion and a sense that life's meaning depends on obedience, and also on vigilance against the enemy'.[2]

The radical multiculturalism of the libertarians, and some on the left, takes a very different line, embracing cultural pluralism at whatever cost to wider solidarity. In this view, national identity has no priority over other cultural claims – indeed, national identity is often regarded as of dubious provenance, as artificially constructed, and as serving the interests of ruling groups.

Cultural pluralism

Now obviously special group affiliations don't necessarily prejudice national identity. Many loyalties that individuals and groups have, such as those to their neighbourhood or religion, don't inevitably clash with national belonging. Because of their inclusive quality, ethnic, and sometimes religious, identities pose the biggest problem. Yet concerning such groups the claims of radical multiculturalism are quite misleading. Ethnic identities aren't any less socially constructed than are national identities – all ethnic identity is the outcome in some part of the use of power and created from diverse cultural sources. In the area of ethnicity, as in nationalism, there are no thoroughbreds. Moreover, radical multiculturalism presumes the very national community it affects to reject. The aim of multiculturalist politics is entirely laudable – to counter the exploitation of oppressed groups. But this cannot be done without the support of the broad national community, or without a sense of social justice that must stretch beyond the claims or grievances of any specific group. 'Much more rests on the majority's sense of fairness than multiculturalists appreciate, and that sense of fairness is liable to be contracted if groups issuing demands reject the identity by which they belong in the same community as the majority.'[3]

It could be argued, of course, that current social trends undermine the possibility of constructing the cosmopolitan nation. Isn't the reality that fragmentation referred to earlier, with national identity falling apart in the face of ethnic tribalism on the one hand

and the regional break-up of states on the other? In Europe, Yugoslavia and Czechoslovakia have been sub-divided. Who knows whether Belgium will hold together, the north of Italy separate from the south or the Basques form a separate state?

Yet all is not fragmentation. In Germany in place of two states there is now one, and the same will probably eventually happen in Korea. 'Tribalism' is decreasing in some areas and contexts rather than growing. The ethnic conflicts in Northern Ireland, for example, are exceptional in Europe, and at the time of writing it seems as though a constitutional settlement which might counter them has been found.

The cosmopolitan nation is an active nation; but nation-building has to have a different sense now from in previous generations, when it was part of a 'realist' system of international relations. Nations in the past were constructed in some large part out of antagonism to others – in the case of Britain, as Linda Colley has shown, hostility to Catholic France.[4] Today, national identities must be sustained in a collaborative milieu, where they won't have the level of inclusiveness they once did, and where other loyalties exist alongside them. What is implied, as elsewhere in society, is a more open and reflexive construction of national identity – which marks out what is distinctive about the nation and its aspirations, but in a less taken-for-granted way than before.

As borders become fuzzier, and claims to local autonomy more insistent, old forms of national identity have to be restructured. The question of 'who are we?' becomes puzzling, yet pushes for a coherent answer.

'Britishness' is as puzzling as any. As the political thinker Bernard Crick remarks, 'I am a citizen of a country with no agreed colloquial name.'[5] Many say 'England' when they mean 'Britain', and sometimes the other way round. 'Britain' is technically not the same as 'Great Britain' (England, Scotland and Wales), or the 'United Kingdom' (Great Britain and Northern Ireland). Devolution will sharpen the national sense of Scotland and Wales – indeed Scotland may well claim full independence. If the settlement there takes effect, Northern Ireland will have links both to Ireland and to the British mainland. Not only all this: Britain has large ethnic and immigrant minorities, a legacy in some part of its imperial past. This heterogeneity may defeat any attempt to reshape an embracing national identity but in and of itself it isn't a barrier. Rather it is part and parcel of the very meaning of 'cosmopolitan nation' as such.

One of the major issues facing many countries is immigration. The US from its beginnings has been an immigrant society. The European countries, however, now have much more heterogeneous populations than they did twenty years ago. Germany, for instance, is an immigrant country in fact if not in name. Its demographic make-up has altered in quite a short time. Four times as many immigrants went to Germany as to France in 1990, and eight times as many as to Britain. Germany accepted 1.1 million immigrants in 1995, while immigration into the US was 720,000.[6]

Immigration has long been fertile soil for racism, in spite of the fact that studies from around the world show that immigration usually proves advantageous to

135

the host country. Immigrants normally want to work and are often more industrious than the indigenous population. They want to prosper and by doing so they become consumers, creating jobs rather than usurping them. The very cultural differences that may cause resentment or hatred tend to have an energizing effect upon the society at large.

The countries which signed the 1985 Schengen agreement to have open borders are calling on EU members with 'external boundaries' to patrol them more rigorously. In June 1998 France sent police reinforcements to its Italian border to prevent Kurdish refugees from entering. Germany demanded road checkpoints be set up in Italy; it has reinforced controls on its borders with Poland. None the less, the Schengen accord has survived the influx of escapees from Yugoslavia and later Albania.

Cosmopolitanism and multiculturalism merge around the question of immigration. A cosmopolitan outlook is the necessary condition of a multicultural society in a globalizing order. Cosmopolitan nationalism is the only form of national identity compatible with that order. Even more than most other countries, Germany is being forced to examine its national identity afresh. It was the only society actually split in two by the bipolar world. The country has to shape a new identity, like others in Europe, while ceding a measure of economic and cultural autonomy to the EU – in which it is first among equals.

Germany is something of a test case for cosmopolitan nationalism in the context of Europe, because the country officially denies its multiculturalism. Natural-

136

ization is currently based on descent, not place of birth. Generations of immigrant children born in Germany remain foreigners, while those of German origins born in other countries may claim German citizenship. To pioneer a cosmopolitan identity, the citizenship laws need to be changed and a major cultural shift made. A cosmopolitan nation needs values to which all are committed, and an identity with which citizens are comfortable, but it also has to accept ambiguity and cultural diversity.

Is benign, cosmopolitan nationalism actually possible? As with other notions discussed earlier, it is an ideal, but given the changing nature of the global order, one not so distant from reality. Talk of Cool Britannia in the UK, and of 'rebranding Britain', fumbling though they might be, mark a recognition that national identity needs to be actively shaped, in dialogue with other identities.

According to 'realist' theory, nations and power blocs, acting in the selfish pursuit of their interests, are the arbiters of power in the world arena. It is obvious, however, that this is a self-defining theory. States' leaders who think in such a way will act in such a way. The end of the bipolar era, together with the impact of globalization, have radically altered the nature of states' sovereignty. Globalization, it should be stressed, is not the same as internationalization. It is not just about closer ties between nations, but concerns processes, such as the emergence of global civil society, that cut across the borders of nations. States which face risks and dangers, rather than enemies, have no need to see the world in realist terms – 'realism' is the wrong term, since the beliefs to which it refers are becoming archaic.

Cosmopolitan democracy

The new democratic state and the cosmopolitan nation are bound up with a much wider political arena that can no longer be treated as merely 'external'. The cosmopolitan nation implies cosmopolitan democracy, operating on a globalizing scale.[7] Now normally such issues are kept quite separate from discussions of national and even regional politics. The rest of the world is far away, it is said, and we have enough troubles in our own back yard, while ideas about democracy above the level of the nation-state are utopian. In academic discourse, this separation has long been formalized by the existence of the discipline of 'international relations', whose province of study is just this 'external arena'. In a globalizing order, however, such a differentiation makes little sense.

Some say that the world is going backwards from global governance, not towards it – the break-up of the bipolar world has generated disorder rather than increasing interdependence. Although he recognizes that 'global chaos is entirely avoidable', journalist Robert Harvey argues that 'as the millennium closes, the . . . seeds of global disorder, even anarchy . . . are being sown'.[8] The French thinker Alain Minc has similarly spoken of the return of a new Middle Ages, characterized by a profusion of conflicts, hostilities and grey areas devoid of authority.[9]

Rather than describing the world as it is, however, which as yet they plainly do not, such interpretations should be seen as dystopias, the catastrophic side of the positive possibilities that exist. Consider, for example, the impact of war. Far more people have died on the battlefield over the past hundred years than in any previous century. If civilian deaths are included, a greater proportion of the world's population died in warfare than at any period before. Some 10 million people perished in fighting in World War I; millions more died directly or indirectly as a result of the war. World War II had a far higher proportion of civilian casualties: of the 50 million who died, under half were soldiers. It has been estimated that a further 50 million people have been killed in other conflicts from 1945 to the present day. In very recent times the bloodshed in Bosnia and Rwanda has added another million victims.[10]

Yet appalling as these last episodes of violence were, they indicate a change in the pattern of war, away from the earlier geopolitical wars of nation-states. The obsolescence of large-scale war, accidents aside, had already become clear during the bipolar era. The invention of nuclear weapons reversed the theorem of Karl von Clausewitz – rather than war being the final instrument of diplomacy, the overriding object of diplomacy became to prevent war, at least in the sense of nuclear conflict. Mikhail Gorbachev explicitly recognized the obsolescence of war in proposing the arms race should come to a halt, a matter of much more than just expediency on his part.[11]

There are several other reasons why it is no longer fanciful to say that large-scale war between nations is less likely to occur in the future. The world is no longer divided between two militarized power blocs. The boundaries between nations have almost everywhere been fixed and agreed by international consensus. In an information age, territory no longer matters as much to nation-states as in the past. Knowledge and competitive capability count for more than natural resources, and sovereignty has become fuzzier or multiple. Democracy is becoming more widespread and there is truth in the idea that democracies do not go to war with one another. Finally, the world is vastly more interconnected than ever before, including the period of the late nineteenth century.

Against this backdrop it is no longer utopian to connect issues of national and global governance, because they are already intimately connected in practice. Underneath the restlessness of markets and the driving force of technological innovation there has been a massive growth in the number of cooperative organizations working at a global level. At the turn of the present century, for example, there were some twenty international governmental organizations and 180 transnational non-government organizations. Today there are over 300 of the former and nearly 5,000 of the latter. There already is global governance and there already is global civil society.[12]

There are major forms of cosmopolitanism coming 'from below'. Groups such as Greenpeace or Amnesty International pursue objectives relating to humanity as a whole. Amnesty International, for instance, follows a principle of 'strict impartiality and independence', ensuring that its members do not become involved in cases in their own countries. NGOs have taken up the rallying call, convening a succession of summit meetings, the largest of which, in Beijing, in 1995 drew 50,000 delegates.

Globalizing processes have transferred powers away from nations and into depoliticized global space. Yet like any other social environment, or even more so given its universal importance, this new space needs regulation, the introduction of rights and obligations: 'ubi societas, ibi ius', 'wherever there is society, there should be laws'.[13]

At present there is a disjunction between regional and global governance. Regionally, especially in the shape of the European Union, NAFTA and other groupings, cooperation is developing in institutions of wide influence. Besides the EU there are the OAU, ASEAN, the League of Arab States, CARICOM and MERCOSUR. All are examples of social and economic collaboration among countries that have had divisions and conflicts in the past. On a truly world level, on the other hand, the existing institutions are still intergovernmental – depending upon the agreement of states to function, they have little power to intervene within them. The UN is specifically an association of nations, as are the bodies concerned with trade and economic exchange – the WTO, GATT, the IMF and the World Bank.

The European Union

The European Union began as part of the bipolar system, but should be understood today as a response to globalization. What matters is not so much that it defines an entity, 'Europe', as that it is developing social, political and economic institutions that stretch above the nation-state and reach down to the individual. Created by cooperation between national governments, it is far more than a regional association of states. Of course, the EU has its problems – it has been said that if it applied to join itself it would be refused entry, because it isn't democratic enough. Yet even in its current form it offers a model capable of wider application, and could play a direct role in providing it.

The EU has become increasingly important in the lives of its citizens at the same time as it is losing popular support. It is responsible for over 75 per cent of economic legislation across its member states, and for 50 per cent of all domestic legislation. However, surveys show that in most member countries there is less enthusiasm for the EU than there used to be – with two or three societies moving the other way. The reasons normally given are the EU's lack of democracy and its remoteness from the concerns of ordinary people. But seen in the context of globalization, and made more responsive to citizens' everyday concerns, the EU is as important for its political role as for its economic one, because in this respect it is ahead of the rest of the world. It is pioneering forms of governance that do not fit any traditional mould. Member countries of the EU have a strong motivation to behave like cosmopolitan nations outside as well as within the European context.

Jos de Beus, author of the 1994 Election Programme

of the Dutch Labour Party, says there are three traps that social democrats should avoid when considering the future of the EU:

- pressure thinking – globalization means that the EU must succumb to pressures from the wider world, rather than seek independently to influence it;
- wishful thinking – the single market, the Euro and the European Central Bank will automatically promote social democratic ideals;
- doomsday thinking – the EU is the enemy of social democracy, so that the aim of social democrats should be to return power to the individual nations.[14]

De Beus is right to suggest that the future of the EU is open. During the Cold War period, the democratic limitations of the EU were not a significant barrier to its evolution. Decisions agreed upon by national governments 'in Brussels' were accepted by voters. In the 1990s this situation no longer holds. Part of the answer, as many suggest, should be to couple greater power for the European Parliament (EP) to more effective transnational party organization. Transnational party federations are likely to get stronger. At present, EP elections are fought as 'second order national contests' rather than 'European elections'. Evidence from polls in different EU countries shows that it is the perceived lack of importance of EP elections that leads people to stay away from the polls.

The projected involvement of countries in Central and Eastern Europe in the EU is obviously a major challenge. The countries lined up for early entry include the Czech Republic, Estonia, Hungary, Poland and Slovenia. Five other countries – Bulgaria, Romania, Slovakia, Latvia and Lithuania – have been allocated resources to help them prepare for entry. Most of these countries have a GDP of a third or less of the existing EU average. Moreover, almost without exception they are struggling to introduce liberal democratic institutions and market principles. Even those that seemed to be making the transition with the greatest ease, such as the Czech Republic and Poland, are meeting problems on both political and economic levels.

The strains that are bound to be caused by 'enlargement' could cause the whole European project to founder. Yet enlargement could help the EU by adding force to processes of reconstruction. After all, as mentioned before, there is more than a faint irony in an undemocratic organization imposing criteria of democracy on others. The incorporation of the societies of Central and Eastern Europe could be a stimulus to democratize and reshape EU institutions. 'If enlargement is to be successful, the EU must address the complex and thorny issues of social and cultural identity, mission and legitimacy and the doubts and anxieties they provoke across Europe.'[15]

Global governance

Whether the basic arrangement of EU institutions will change substantially over the next few years we do not know. The division of powers in the EU may need major restructuring in the light of the issues just mentioned. But it is also possible that a more comprehensive system of global governance could have the same formal system as the EU already possesses: a representative body (the Parliament), an administrative one (the Commission), an intergovernmental association (the Council) and federal courts of law (the Court of Justice). Such an alignment of institutions on a global level, of course, would differ in role and function from the bodies that exist at the moment. In principle, however, it isn't difficult to see how they could be reformed in this direction. For example, the WTO, IMF and World Bank could be integrated as a single body, while what is currently the UN could be divided into a parliament and a council. The OECD might even be a possible bridgehead to a wider global order, if it absorbed the European Union and extended the same powers as the EU already holds to the other members. For the countries of the South, this could be a positive move, because it would no longer be an exclusive club, but a group with membership available to all those who qualify.

The idea that a new assembly, or parliament, could be set up in conjunction with the UN has been widely debated over the past few years.[16] The European Parliament could be a model for how such a parliamentary assembly could be formed. It could be established initially as a subsidiary body of the General Assembly, under article 22 of the UN charter. Parliaments of the member states would first of all send representatives who would develop proposals for a directly elected assembly. The electoral system would be similar to that of the European Parliament, with the number of deputies from each country proportionate to population, with a corrective built in for smaller countries.[17]

The development of an effective court of justice would be a crucial step accompanying a world assembly. The International Court of Justice continues to represent an intergovernmental conception of law, in spite of the fact that the Nuremberg and Tokyo Tribunals established a principle of jurisdiction over individuals and their states. The tribunal set up to investigate and prosecute violations of international human rights law in the former Yugoslavia has analogous powers. It could, and should, form a link to a framework of cosmopolitan law, the basic issue in which is that the court's jurisdiction should extend widely over relations between states and their citizens. The fact that most states as of 1998 have supported the formation of an International Criminal Court is a sign of a gathering consensus about these needs.

Are such proposals feasible? Would globalized democracy, featuring representative assemblies, meet with the same problems of apathy or hostility encountered at the national level? As far as the second question is concerned, it is essential to emphasize again the two-way diffusion of power. Cosmopolitan democracy is not only about the movement of governance towards a world level, but about its diffusion downwards to local regions. Those who doubt such possibilities should consider what has been achieved in the European Union. Only half a century ago Europe was exhausted, recovering from a war coming from long-standing tensions between the European states. Yet those states have collaborated to create a new system of transnational and devolved power, have pooled aspects of their sovereignty and have set up effective courts of law. They have done so, moreover, not just out of idealism, but out of self-interest, and similar interests in global governance are today relevant to all states.[18]

The expansion of cosmopolitan democracy is a condition for effectively regulating the world economy, attacking global economic inequalities and controlling ecological risks. It makes no sense to contest market fundamentalism on the local level but leave it to reign on the global one:

> Global laissez-faire is a moment in the history of the emerging world economy, not its end point ... what is beyond serious doubt is that organising the world economy as a single global free market promotes instability. It forces workers to bear the cost of new technologies and unrestricted free trade. It contains no means whereby activities that endanger the global ecological balance can be curbed . . . [It] is, in effect, staking the planet's future on the supposition that these vast dangers will be resolved as an unintended consequence of the unaffected pursuit of profits. It is hard to think of a more reckless wager.[19]

Market fundamentalism on a world scale

Market fundamentalism has been forced into retreat in domestic politics because of its limited and contradictory nature. Yet it still continues to reign at a global

147

level, in spite of the fact that the same problems appear there as more locally. In neoliberal orthodoxy, giving global markets free reign is logical, because like all markets they are problem-solving devices and tend towards equilibrium. Seemingly irrational fluctuations are actually condensed problem-solving activities, reverting very soon to a new and readjusted equilibrium. A more convincing account of the dynamics of world markets, however, suggests that expectations of price changes rather than prices as such drive decisions, and expectations are routinely swayed by psychological rather than purely economic phenomena. Crises, erratic fluctuations, the sudden rush of capital into and out of particular countries and regions – these are not marginal but core features of untamed markets.

The regulation of financial markets is the single most pressing issue in the world economy, in the wake of the Mexican crisis of 1994 and the succeeding troubles in South East Asia. Here as elsewhere deregulation isn't the same as freedom, and a global commitment to free trade depends upon effective regulation rather than dispenses with the need for it. The aims of such intervention are easy to identify, but what policies should be followed, and how they can be implemented, obviously are more problematic. The needs are: to calm excessive movements in currencies and control overshoot; separate short-term currency speculation from investment; and create greater accountability within the transnational organizations involved in world economic management, as well as restructure them.

Of the trillion US dollars' worth of currencies exchanged every day, only 5 per cent relate to trade and other substantive economic transactions. The other 95 per cent is made up of speculations and arbitrages, as traders wielding huge sums look for rapid profits on exchange rate fluctuations and interest rate differentials. These activities distort the signals markets give for long-term instruments and trade. Portfolio capital has spectacular mobility – hundreds of billions of 'hot money' can desert a market or country in one day. Central banks don't have sufficient reserves to withstand the collective pressure of speculators gambling on the devaluation of weaker currencies.

Following the Mexican crisis, many wrote of the need to create more effective instruments of financial governance – but few substantive changes were put in place. The dislocations suffered by the Asian tiger economies have made much more apparent the need for new modes of regulation. After all, the Asian countries went from being models of industrial success to struggling economies almost overnight. Prior to these events, it wasn't so obvious that movements of capital could so readily generate crises. In 1996, $93 billion flowed into Indonesia, South Korea, Malaysia, Thailand and the Philippines. Suddenly in 1997 this went into reverse, with an outflow of $12 billion.[20]

The neoliberal response, to free up capital markets still further, is only a recipe for even greater dislocation than has been suffered over the past few years. The idea that controlling the free mobility of capital produces losses of efficiency takes no account of the social and economic costs of crises. Ensuring that capital returns usually means raising interest rates and selling domestic assets. Moreover, the claims often made for the benefits of free capital mobility are at least questionable. China and Japan, among other countries, have had high growth rates without capital account convertibility. In Europe, the same has been true of Ireland and Portugal, which did not move fully in this direction until the early 1990s.

How might financial markets be regulated? One key aspect is currency speculation. The coming of the Euro means there will be three world currencies, with a question mark hanging over the yen. This situation could lead to struggles between the currency blocs, but also implies a growing coordination in the world economy that could turn into active cooperation. The financier George Soros has suggested that the Euro and the US dollar could be formally linked as a stabilizing device.

Stable exchange rates should benefit financial institutions, corporations, investors and governments alike. Longer-term investment and lending are encouraged by more stability. Costs to exporters and importers will be lower, because the need to hedge against exchange rate fluctuations will not be there. Moreover, industrialized and developing countries alike stand to gain, since both seek more government autonomy and effective central bank intervention.

An alternative to a fixed exchange rate regime is the much-discussed Tobin tax, which its originator suggested over a quarter of a century ago.[21] The tax would be set at a level that would discourage pure financial speculation, while not preventing currency exchange necessary for the finance of trade and direct investment. A tax of 0.5 per cent applied in 1996 would have produced $150 billion if levied on a world scale. Critics claim that it would not be workable, because traders would find ways to evade it. The main barrier, however, does not concern problems of evasion, or implementation more generally, but – so far – lack of political will. On a more local level, the reserve system in Chile has deservedly attracted much attention. Those who wish to invest in the country are obliged to make a substantial deposit, at zero interest, with the central bank for a period of a year, the effect being to separate genuine investment from more speculative financial dealings.

The World Bank, IMF and GATT were set up to cope with the global dislocations of the 1920s and 1930s, not those of today. The Bretton Woods – GATT system was introduced to avoid the difficulties that arose after World War I, including restrictive trade policies and the Great Depression – the period commonly known as 'the age of catastrophe'. The aim was to encourage international economic cooperation through an expanding and open world economy. These objectives have largely been achieved. Virulent economic nationalism has not reappeared and no major wars have happened between the countries at the core of the system. In some part it is that very success that has generated a whole new series of problems.

Serious consideration should be given to establishing an Economic Security Council within the United Nations. To do so would be as difficult as other reforms, or more so, but it would be hard to dispute its importance. It would require a change in the charter of the UN and 'a political will of heroic proportions'.[22]

151

G8 could continue to play its current role in coordinating the policy frameworks of the industrial countries. There are many issues, including governance of currency markets and responding to ecological risks, that cannot be resolved without collective action involving many countries and groups. Not even the most liberalized national economy works without macroeconomic coordination; it makes no sense to suppose that the world economy is different.

The issue of global ecological management overlaps extensively with that of the deep economic divisions in world society. There is a real parallel between exclusion within nations and regions and exclusion on a global scale. Increasing prosperity for many leaves others stranded and marginalized. The richest twenty countries in the world have experienced a steady advance in prosperity since 1980. About a quarter of the world's population lives in these countries. Economic stagnation, or even absolute decline, has characterized many of the poorer societies. About 30 per cent of the world's population lives on a poverty line of earnings equivalent to one US dollar a day. Sub-Saharan Africa, with the partial exception of South Africa, makes up virtually a whole continent of the excluded. Even among poor countries there is exclusion at the top as well. Small elites, sometimes affluent by any standards, live in physical and cultural isolation from the large majority. Quite often they are openly getting their income from money laundering, weapons trading or drug trafficking.

The problems involved in reducing world inequality are truly daunting. It seems very unlikely, however, that a significant impact could be made on them without progress towards greater global governance. The same applies to ecological risk. The question isn't only how environmental threats can be contained, but the effects of the economic development of the poorer countries, supposing it occurs. Ecological modernization, as currently understood, does not provide strategies for the transition from an agrarian to an industrial economy. World ecological management, to say the least, will not be easy, not just because of pressures towards environmentally damaging economic growth, but because ecological risks, and more broadly those associated with technological change, are intrinsically so controversial.

Accusations of unnecessary scaremongering don't only come from the right, and many people lapse into the view that 'things will work out in the end'. Since by definition no one can calculate the risks, and future technological change is impossible to predict, no fully convincing scenarios can be drawn. Global problems respond to local initiatives but they also demand global solutions. We can't leave such problems to the erratic swirl of global markets and relatively powerless international bodies if we are to achieve a world that mixes stability, equity and prosperity.

Conclusion

In the early 1990s contributors to the discussion about the future of social democracy spoke of the air of disappointment that has surrounded social democratic renewal.[1] Social democrats across Europe, and in other areas of the world too, lost confidence in the face of the rise of free market philosophy and the collapse of 'actually existing socialism' in Eastern Europe. Ronald Reagan and George Bush held power in the US, while two of the major social democratic parties, in Britain and Germany, experienced long periods of opposition. Although social democrats did well in Southern Europe, electorally as well as conceptually 'social democracy fell into a state of depression'.[2]

A number of key events, including the election to the US presidency of Bill Clinton in 1992, helped turn the tide. Wim Kok became prime minister in Holland, Lionel Jospin came to power in France, Romano Prodi in Italy. The victory of Labour in the UK was also seen in many countries as a new beginning. 'And then there was Tony!', proclaimed the authors of a volume on the

154

state of social democracy in Europe in 1998, adding that Tony Blair defeated 'the very symbol of the social democratic crisis of the 80s, Thatcherite conservatism'.[3]

Yet many who praise the scale of the victory also see the New Labour project as an empty one. The landslide majority New Labour achieved was the result of a very active, professional campaign, in which media techniques developed in the US were utilized. New Labour is widely seen as depending on media-oriented politics, and as creating 'designer socialism'. 'Personal images, symbolic stagings, sound bites, visual gags' all count for more than 'issues, arguments, projects and the evaluation of campaign promises.'[4]

A precept of successful advertising, however, is that image alone isn't enough. There must be something solid behind the hype, otherwise the public see through the façade pretty quickly. If all New Labour had to offer were media savvy, its time on the political stage would be short, and its contribution to the revival of social democracy limited. I hope this will not be the case. As I have tried to show in this book, a substantive agenda is emerging from the social democratic debates, an agenda to which the UK has a lot to offer. The more these debates themselves become genuinely transnational the better. Even within Europe, there hasn't been as much interaction across national contexts as there might be. But a dialogue of the centre-left should range much more widely, as an orientation to globalization in fact demands.

Notes

Preface

[1] David Marquand: 'The Blair paradox', *Prospect*, May 1998, p. 20.

Chapter 1   Socialism and After

[1] Tony Blair, interview, *Guardian*, 7 February 1998.
[2] E.F.M. Durbin: *Problems of Economic Planning*. London: Routledge, 1949, p. 41.
[3] Fritz W. Scharpf: 'Flexible integration', in Ian Christie: *EuroVisions*. London: Demos, 1998.
[4] David Green: *Reinventing Civil Society*. London: Institute of Economic Affairs, 1993, p. viii.
[5] John Gray: *Enlightenment's Wake*. London: Routledge, 1997, p. 103.
[6] David Marsland: *Welfare or Welfare State?*. Basingstoke: Macmillan, 1996, p. 212.
[7] Marsland: *Welfare or Welfare State?*, p. 197.
[8] Egon Matzner and Wolfgang Streeck: *Beyond Keynesianism*. Aldershot: Elgar, 1991, pp. 3–4.
[9] Herbert Kitschelt: *The Transformation of European Social Democracy*. Cambridge: Cambridge University Press, 1994, p. 33.
[10] Knut Heidar: 'The Norwegian labour party', in Richard Gillespie and William E. Paterson: *Rethinking Social Democracy in Europe*. London: Cass, 1993, p. 62.

[11] Quoted in Stephen Padgett: 'The German Social Democrats', in Gillespie and Paterson: *Rethinking Social Democracy*, pp. 27 and 29.

[12] Ulrich Beck: 'The reinvention of politics', in Ulrich Beck, Anthony Giddens and Scott Lash: *Reflexive Modernization*. Cambridge: Polity Press, 1994.

[13] Inglehart's work has generated numerous critiques and evaluations. For a useful summary, see Clive Bean and Elim Papadakis: 'Polarised priorities or flexible alternatives?', *International Journal of Public Opinion Research*, vol. 6, no. 3, 1997.

[14] John Blundell and Brian Gosschalk: *Beyond Left and Right*. London: Institute of Economic Affairs, 1997.

[15] Robert Worcester: 'Introduction', in Blundell and Gosschalk: *Beyond Left and Right*, p. 3.

[16] Kitschelt: *Transformation of European Social Democracy*, p. 33.

[17] Kurt Sontheimer, quoted in Padgett: 'German social democrats', p. 38. For the recent discussion in the UK, see the interesting contributions to the Nexus 'virtual think-tank', reprinted in book form as David Halpern and David Mikosz: *The Third Way*. London: Nexus, 1998.

Chapter 2   Five Dilemmas

[1] Pervenche Beres: 'The social democratic response to globalisation', in René Cuperus and Johannes Kandel: *European Social Democracy: Transformation in Progress*. Amsterdam: Friedrich Ebert Stiftung, 1998.

[2] Kenichi Ohmae: *The End of the Nation State: The Rise of Regional Economies*. London: HarperCollins, 1995.

[3] Paul Hirst and Graham Thompson: *Globalization in Question*. Cambridge: Polity Press, 1996, p. 1.

[4] David Held: 'Democracy and globalization', in Daniele Archibugi, David Held and Martin Kohler: *Re-Imagining Political Community*. Cambridge: Polity Press, 1998.

[5] Jeffrey R. Gates: *The Ownership Solution*. New York: Basic Books, 1998, pp. 2 and 36.

[6] Helen Wilkinson and Geoff Mulgan: *Freedom's Children*. London: Demos, 1995.

[7] Ulrich Beck: 'The cosmopolitan manifesto', *New Statesman*, 20 March 1998.

[8] Zeev Sternhell: *Ni droite ni gauche*. Paris: Seuil, 1983.

[9] Quoted in Donald Sassoon: *One Hundred Years of Socialism*. London: Tauris, 1996, p. 776.

[10] Norberto Bobbio: *Left and Right*. Cambridge: Polity Press, 1996.

[11] Bobbio: *Left and Right*, p. 16.

[12] Bobbio: 'Reply to the critics', in *Left and Right*, p. 133.

[13] Joseph Raz: *The Morality of Freedom*. Oxford: Clarendon Press, 1986, p. 86.

[14] Anthony Giddens: *Beyond Left and Right*. Cambridge: Polity Press, 1994.

[15] J.K. Galbraith: *The Culture of Contentment*. London: Sinclair–Stevenson, 1992.

[16] Ulrich Beck: *The Risk Society*. London: Sage, 1992.

[17] Shell: *Profits and Principles*. London: Shell, 1998.

[18] Ulrich Beck: 'The reinvention of politics', in Ulrich Beck, Anthony Giddens and Scott Lash: *Reflexive Modernization*. Cambridge: Polity Press, 1994, pp. 17–19.

[19] Quoted in Beck: 'The reinvention of politics', p. 22.

[20] University of Washington Graduate School of Public Affairs: Trust in Government Project. Seattle, 1998.

[21] Joseph Nye: 'In government we don't trust', *Foreign Policy*, Fall 1997.

[22] Ferdinand Müller-Rommel: 'The new challengers: greens and right-wing populist parties in Western Europe', *European Review*, vol. 6, 1998, p. 201.

[23] Andrei Markovits and Philip Gorski: *The German Left*. Cambridge: Polity Press, 1993; New York: Oxford

University Press, 1993, p. 269.

24 Julian L. Simon and Herman Kahn: *The Resourceful Earth*. Oxford: Blackwell, 1984.

25 World Commission on Environment and Development: *Our Common Future*. Oxford: Oxford University Press, 1987, p. 8.

26 Maarten A. Hajer: *The Politics of Environmental Discourse*. Oxford: Clarendon Press, 1995.

27 John Dryzek: *The Politics of the Earth*. Oxford: Oxford University Press, 1997, p. 145.

28 Beck: 'The reinvention of politics', p. 29.

29 Julian Le Grand: 'Knights, knaves or pawns', *Journal of Social Policy*, vol. 26, part 2, April 1997.

Chapter 3   State and Civil Society

1 Joseph Nye: 'In government we don't trust', *Foreign Policy*, Fall 1997.

2 E.J. Dionne: *They Only Look Dead*. New York: Simon and Schuster, 1996, p. 290.

3 David Osborne and Ted Gaebler: *Reinventing Government*. Reading: Addison-Wesley, 1992.

4 Will Hutton: *The State We're In*. London: Cape, 1995, p. 293.

5 Robert Wuthnow: *Sharing the Journey*. New York: Free Press, 1994, p. 12.

6 Peter Hall: 'Social capital in Britain'. Mimeo, Center for European Studies, Harvard University, 1997.

7 Anne Power: *Estates on the Edge*. London: Macmillan, 1997.

8 Judith Tendler: *Good Government in the Tropics*. Baltimore: Johns Hopkins University Press, 1997.

9 Emile Durkheim, in Anthony Giddens: *Durkheim on Politics and the State*. Cambridge: Polity Press, 1986, p. 57.

10 George L. Kelling and Catherine M. Coles: *Fixing Broken Windows*. New York: Simon and Schuster, 1997, p. 20.

[11] Stephen L. Carter: *Civility*. New York: Basic Books, 1998.

[12] Kelling and Coles: *Fixing Broken Windows*, pp. 234–5.

[13] Judith Stacey: 'Transatlantic traffic in the politics of family values'. Mimeo, University of California, 1997, p. 4.

[14] Sara McLanahan and Gary Sandefur: *Growing Up with a Single Parent*. Cambridge, Mass.: Harvard University Press, 1994, p. 1.

[15] Adrienne Burgess: *Fatherhood Reclaimed*. London: Vermilion, 1997, pp. 214–17.

[16] Adrienne Burgess: *A Complete Parent*. London: IPPR, 1998.

[17] W.J. Doherty: 'The best of times and the worst of times', in A.J. Hawkins and D.C. Dollahite: *Generative Fathering*. London: Sage, 1997.

[18] Daniel Callahan: *Setting Limits*. New York: Simon and Schuster, 1987.

Chapter 4   The Social Investment State

[1] Robert H. Frank and Philip J. Cook: *The Winner-Take-All Society*. New York: Free Press, 1995.

[2] Christopher Lasch: *The Revolt of the Elites*. New York: Norton, 1995.

[3] Anne Power: *Estates on the Edge*. London: Macmillan, 1997.

[4] Mickey Kaus: *The End of Equality*. New York: Basic Books, 1992.

[5] Alan Wolfe: *One Nation, After All*. New York: Viking, 1998, p. 237.

[6] Wolfe: *One Nation, After All*, p. 248.

[7] *Report of the Social Justice Commission*. London: Vintage, 1994, p. 175.

[8] John Walsh: *Stories of Renewal: Community Building and the Future of Urban America*. Report to the Rockefeller Foundation, 1996.

[9] Nicholas Timmins: *The Five Giants*. London: Fontana, 1996, p. 12.

[10] Kees van Kersbergen: *Social Capitalism*. London: Routledge, 1995, p. 7.

[11] Howard Glennerster and John Hills: *The State of Welfare*. 2nd edition. Oxford: Oxford University Press, 1998.

[12] Assar Lindbeck: 'The end of the middle way?', *American Economic Review*, vol. 85, 1995.

[13] Peter Baldwin: *The Politics of Social Solidarity*. Cambridge: Cambridge University Press, 1990, p. 292.

[14] Stuart Fleming: 'What we'll earn when we're 64', *New Statesman*, 5 June 1998.

[15] Will Hutton: *The State We're In*. London: Cape, 1995.

[16] Edmund Burke: *Reflections on the Revolution in France*. London: Dent, 1910, pp. 93–4.

[17] Daniel Callahan: *Setting Limits*. New York: Simon and Schuster, 1987, p. 46.

[18] Callahan: *Setting Limits*, p. 20.

[19] Stephen Nickell: 'Unemployment and labour market rigidities', *Journal of Economic Perspectives*, vol. 11, 1997.

[20] Dominic Vidal: 'Miracle or mirage in the Netherlands?', *Le Monde Diplomatique*, July 1997.

[21] Rosabeth Moss Kanter: 'Keynote address', Centre for Economic Performance: Employability and Exclusion. London: CEP, May 1998.

[22] Moss Kanter: 'Keynote address', pp. 65–8.

[23] Ulrich Beck: 'Capitalism without work', *Dissent*, Winter 1997, p. 102.

[24] Jeremy Rifkin: *The End of Work*. New York: Putnam's, 1995, p. 225.

[25] Beck: 'Capitalism without work', p. 106.

Chapter 5   Into the Global Age

[1] David Miller: *On Nationalism*. Oxford: Clarendon Press, 1995, pp. 416 and 420.

[2] Roger Scruton: 'In defence of the nation', in *The Philo-*

sopher on Dover Beach. Manchester: Carcanet, 1990, p. 310.

3 Miller: *On Nationalism*, p. 140.

4 Linda Colley: *Britons*. New Haven, Conn.: Yale University Press, 1992.

5 Bernard Crick: 'The English and the British', in *National Identities*. Oxford: Blackwell, 1991, p. 90.

6 Hermann Strasser: 'The German debate over multicultural society', *Canadian Journal of Sociology*, vol. 22, 1997.

7 For the development of the idea of cosmopolitan democracy I am greatly indebted to the writings of David Held, its main pioneer. See in particular *Democracy and the Global Order*. Cambridge: Polity Press, 1995.

8 Robert Harvey: *The Return of the Strong*. London: Macmillan, 1995, p. xv.

9 Alain Minc: *Le nouveau moyen âge*. Paris: Gallimard, 1993.

10 John Keegan: *War and Our World*. London: Hutchinson, 1998, p. 3.

11 Mike McGwire: *Perestroika and Soviet National Security*. New York: Bookings, 1991.

12 David Held et al.: *Global Transformations: Politics, Economy and Culture*. Cambridge: Polity Press, forthcoming.

13 Alberto Tita: 'Globalisation: a new political and economic space, requiring supranational governance'. Mimeo, Università Cattolica del Sacro Cuore, 1998, p. 2.

14 Jos de Beus: 'Modernised social democracy and the fundamental democratisation of Europe', in René Cuperus and Johannes Kandel: *European Social Democracy: Transformation in Progress*. Amsterdam: Friedrich Ebert Stiftung, 1998.

15 Mark Leonard: *Rediscovering Europe*. London: Demos, 1998.

16 Daniele Archibugi, David Held and Martin Kohler: *Re-*

Imagining Political Community. Cambridge: Polity Press, 1998, p. 141.

[17] E. Childers and B. Urquhart, *Renewing the United Nation System.* Uppsala: Dag Hammarskjöld Foundation, 1994, p. 297.

[18] Fred Halliday: 'Global governance – prospects and problems', *Citizenship Studies*, vol. 4, no. 1, forthcoming.

[19] John Gray: *False Dawn.* London: Granta, 1998, pp. 199–200.

[20] Jagdish Bhagwati: 'The capital myth', *Foreign Affairs*, vol. 77, 1998.

[21] Mahbub ul Haq et al.: *The Tobin Tax.* Oxford: Oxford University Press, 1996.

[22] Mahbub ul Haq: 'The case for an economic security council in the United Nations', in Albert J. Paolini et al.: *Between Sovereignty and Global Governance.* London: Macmillan, 1998, p. 229.

Conclusion

[1] Richard Gillespie: 'A programme for social democratic revival?', in Richard Gillespie and William E. Paterson: *Rethinking Social Democracy in Western Europe.* London: Cass, 1993.

[2] René Cuperus and Johannes Kandel: 'The magical return of social democracy', in *European Social Democracy: Transformation in Progress.* Amsterdam: Friedrich Ebert Stiftung, 1998, p. 13.

[3] Cuperus and Kandel: 'The magical return of social democracy', pp. 13 and 15.

[4] Thomas Meyer: 'Basic values, communication and party organisation', in Cuperus and Kandel: *European Social Democracy*, p. 259.

Index

164

Index

Index